Anonymous

The Religious Census of London

Anonymous

The Religious Census of London

ISBN/EAN: 9783337429287

Printed in Europe, USA, Canada, Australia, Japan

Cover: Foto ©Lupo / pixelio.de

More available books at **www.hansebooks.com**

THE
RELIGIOUS CENSUS
OF
LONDON.

Reprinted from "*THE BRITISH WEEKLY.*"

London:
HODDER AND STOUGHTON,
27, PATERNOSTER ROW.
MDCCCLXXXVIII.

INTRODUCTION.

THE following book contains the results of a religious census of London, taken in two parts at the instance of the proprietors of THE BRITISH WEEKLY. The first part contains the results of an enumeration of the worshippers at the two principal services in the churches and chapels of London. While similar enumerations have been made for all the greater cities of the empire, the enormous labour and cost involved in satisfactorily dealing with the problem in London had hitherto proved an insuperable barrier. Some fifteen hundred places, contained within a very wide area, had to be dealt with, and the number of persons employed amounted to several thousands. Thanks to the labours of the general superintendent, Major Colquhoun, of Lyons, who had previously superintended a similar, but much smaller, work in Glasgow; the superintendents of districts, many of them well known in the Christian world; the sub-superintendents, and enumerators; who in the vast majority of cases did their work with the utmost efficiency, the labour has now been accomplished. The day—the 24th of October, 1886—

was bright, though cold, and there is every reason to believe that there was fully an average attendance. Of course in many cases allowance had to be made for various facts. The census does not take account of extra services, and exceptional circumstances in the case of separate churches increased or diminished the attendance for the day. For example, in the Church of England many harvest festivals were held, and in the case of several Nonconformist churches anniversary services were conducted. Sometimes, in various cases of course, the regular ministers were absent. I had hoped to indicate these circumstances more precisely than has been found possible; but I believe implicit reliance may be placed on the accuracy of the figures. They were published by instalments. The enumeration was made by actual counting, official estimates being in no case accepted when unconfirmed, and challenge of specific figures was invited. On due cause shown the matter was investigated, and in a few cases, very small in proportion to the whole number, corrections were made. I have to acknowledge with gratitude the generosity with which the enterprise was commented on by the religious press generally, and I print a few representative letters received from eminent public men. I do not think it advisable to reproduce the articles in which I drew what appeared to me fair inferences from the figures, as the object of this publication is to place the facts before readers and allow them to draw their own conclusions. I may, however, say that the object of the census was in no way sectarian or political, and that many prominent members of all churches took part in it.

From the Right Hon. W. E. Gladstone, M.P.

As one of the public, Mr Gladstone feels much indebted to the Editor, especially in the present very defective state of our information, for the religious census of London.

A numerical comparison with the results obtained in the other great towns would be interesting.

So, of course, would be a comparison with corresponding parts abroad; but this, Mr. Gladstone supposes, would be difficult of attainment.

It occurs to him that perhaps in the United States there might be a disposition to follow the example so well set here.

With Mr. Gladstone's compliments.

December 18th, 1886.

From the Bishop of Wakefield (then Bishop of Bedford).
Stainforth House, Upper Clapton, London, E.
December 17th, 1886.

Sir,—We all owe you a great debt of gratitude for the census of attendance at public worship, which you have made with so much pains, and with such an evident desire to be strictly accurate. Such a laborious work could not be carried out without some errors or omissions; but these seem to me comparatively few, and will, I have no doubt, be corrected when the result of your labour appears in a final form. I think the result is distinctly encouraging, and I heartily sympathise with your hopeful deduction from the statistics you have collected. I have never myself taken a desponding view, but have believed what you press upon us—namely, that the evangelisation of London is not an impossiblity. Thank God, there are evident signs of a more friendly attitude towards religion. But the achievement we hope and pray and labour for is only to be attained by the most earnest and zealous and self-denying exertions of Christian people. If there is much to make us sad and anxious, you have, at least, shown us much to stimulate and encourage.

WM. WALSHAM BEDFORD.
(Bishop Suffragan for East London.)

From the Ven. Archdeacon Farrar, D.D., F.R.S.

December 20th, 1886.

Dr. Farrar has read with great interest the results of the religious census, and the candid and valuable comments made upon them. He is much obliged to the Editor for the copy of last week's issue, and congratulates him on having been able to carry out so arduous an inquiry. The Editor has rendered a valuable service to the whole religious community.

From the Rev. Dr. Thain Davidson.

11, ST. MARY'S ROAD, CANONBURY, N.
December 20th, 1886.

DEAR SIR,—In reply to your note, permit me to express my belief that while these statistics are not so satisfactory as one might have hoped for, their publication will do good by drawing more earnest attention to the practical irreligiousness (I would not use the word *heathenism*) existing in the Metropolis—an irreligiousness due, I am persuaded, to indifference, and consisting only in very small degree of avowed infidelity.

There are two remarks I feel inclined to make upon the religious census just taken. In the first place, these figures must not be held to represent the total influence of Christianity in the midst of us. As one who for twenty-five years has been labouring in London, I am bound to say that I perceive a very great difference in the attitude of the humbler classes towards religion, even amongst those who rarely or never enter our churches.

The cynical contempt or malevolent hate which a minister of the

Gospel would meet with in certain districts some years ago, is now exchanged for a respectful bearing; and working men are beginning to see that they have no better friends than those who are endeavouring to disseminate the principles of our holy faith.

In the second place, may I venture the opinion in regard to the aggregate numbers, as shown by your returns, to be found on a given Sunday within the various places of worship, that they represent nearly all the moral, and to a large extent also the intellectual, force of the Metropolis.

If we put these two considerations together, on each of which a great deal might be said, we shall have little difficulty in coming to the conclusion that, for all that pessimists allege, London is a city dominated by Christianity.

Yours faithfully,
J. THAIN DAVIDSON.

FROM MR. G. HOWELL, M.P.
HAMPDEN HOUSE, ELLINGHAM ROAD,
SHEPHERD'S BUSH, LONDON, W.
December 18th, 1886.

DEAR SIR,—I thank you for the copy of THE BRITISH WEEKLY, with condensed census of the attendances at churches and chapels in the Metropolis. Taking it as a whole, the figures are not discouraging, but I fear that the absentees are more numerous than you assume.

But even were not this the case, there is another aspect of the question which deserves a thought—namely, that the absentees are men in a larger proportion than women. Men will and do attend and in some congregations they form a fair proportion to the whole, but not usually. They are not attracted by *mere* scholarship, but by healthy, manly teaching. Men could be named who will draw large assemblies of men, and hold them to their duties; but they are the exception rather than the rule.

In my opinion, the thing wanted in our ministers of all denominations is intense human sympathy; the more intense, if real, the better. This phase of Christian worship and preaching has developed immensely of late years, and hence there is a growth of religious communities throughout London. There are signs that it is further developing— broadly and healthfully. The more closely Christian ministers follow in the footsteps of Christ, and His followers during His stay, the more surely will Christianity spread.

The social fabric of society has broken down. Political economy has not yet shown how the masses of the people are to be improved, their condition ameliorated, and their health and happiness secured. What is true in economical science can be hallowed by the application to it of the precepts of Christianity, as a living force and vital principle. The very failure of political and social expediencies throws the people back upon Christian doctrines and religious truth. Wisely enforced, these cannot fail them, and they will appeal to their consciences with all the greater force because of the failures alluded to.

The facts you have elicited and published are of great value, and I thank you for them.

Yours faithfully,
GEORGE HOWELL.

The enormous extent of the work prevented a census being taken of the mission halls on the same day. That census was taken on the last Sunday of November, 1887. In this case the returns were furnished by the parties in charge of the halls. The result was a very keen discussion on how far mission halls were successful. I think it advisable in this case also to leave out all controversial matters, and to confine this publication simply to a record of facts, procured at great labour and expense, and as accurate as they can be made.

They will, no doubt, long be the basis of all discussion on the religious condition of London, and will afford a valuable test of the progress made by Christian churches.

I have to acknowledge the very valuable assistance of the late Mr. George J. Stevenson, M.A., in preparing this volume for the press. Mr. Stevenson's acquaintance with the religious condition of London was perhaps unrivalled, and his accuracy is universally known.

THE EDITOR OF "THE BRITISH WEEKLY."

27, PATERNOSTER ROW,
    LONDON, E.C., 1888.

The Census includes morning and evening attendance in what is known as "Smaller London." The population of "Smaller London" in 1881 amounted to 3,816,483. It is estimated at the present at about 4,100,000. It includes 29 Registration Districts: Kensington, Fulham, Chelsea, St. George Hanover Square, Westminster, Marylebone, Hampstead, St. Pancras, Islington, Hackney, St. Giles, Strand, Holborn, London City, Shoreditch, Bethnal Green, Whitechapel, St. George-in-the-East, Stepney, Mile-end, and Poplar in Middlesex; St. Saviour Southwark, St. Olave Southwark, Lambeth, Wandsworth, and Camberwell in Surrey; and Greenwich, Lewisham, and Woolwich in Kent.

The fact that in many churches and chapels services of a special character were held on the day when our census was taken has to some extent affected the attendance at those places, as well as at others in the locality; and it may be well to state that an asterisk (*) affixed to figures indicates that on Census Sunday Anniversary Services or a Harvest Festival were held; and in a few cases services were held in schoolrooms. It should also be stated, that in many places, both churches and chapels, considerable numbers of school-children formed part of the counted congregation, whilst in many other places a separate service was held in schoolrooms for the children, who did not come under the notice of the enumerators. In many Roman Catholic churches services were held at the hours of seven, eight, nine, and ten o'clock, attended by persons who could not attend services at later hours. These persons would treble the number of those present at High Mass, and evening service; only those two services were counted.

CENSUS

OF

MORNING AND EVENING ATTENDANCES

IN THE

CHURCHES AND CHAPELS OF LONDON,

Sunday, October 24th, 1886.

CITY OF LONDON.

Church of England—   *M.*   *E.*

	M.	E.
St. Botolph, Aldgate	531	201
St. Botolph, Bishopsgate Without (*Rev. W. Rogers*)	266	324
St. Bartholomew, Moor-lane (*Rev. W. Denton*)	100	84
St. Botolph, Aldersgate (*Rev. S. F. Jones*)	134	115
St. Giles, Cripplegate Without (*Rev. P. P. Gilbert*)	488	251
St. Thomas, Charterhouse, Goswell-road (*Rev. H. Swann.*)	*441	621
St. Bartholomew-the-Great, West Smithfield (*Rev. W. Pankridge.*)	67	105
St. Sepulchre, Holborn Viaduct (*Rev. J. Jackson*)	162	279
Holy Trinity, Gough-square (*Rev. H. C. Heaton*)	140	160
St. Andrew, Holborn Viaduct (*Rev. H. G. S. Blunt*)	452	480
St. Dunstan-in-the-West, Fleet-street (*Rev. W. Martin*)	189	246
Temple Church (*Rev. Dr. Vaughan*)	676	*a371
All Hallows, Lombard-street (*Rev. C. Mackenzie*)	67	46
All Hallows, Barking (*Rev. A. J. Mason*)	134	140
All Hallows-the-Great and Less (*Rev. J. R. Stock*)	59	48
Christ Church, Newgate-street (*Rev. T. D. Cox Morse.*)	*851	69
St. Alban, Wood-street, Cheapside (*Rev. W. A. Carter*)	105	31
St. Alphage, London-wall (*Rev. R. W. Bush*)	77	68
St. Andrew-by-ye-Wardrobe (*Rev. Percival Clement Smith.*)	140	*132
SS. Ann and Agnes (*Rev. J. W. Reynolds*)	42	22
SS. Augustine and Faith, Old Change (*Rev. W. H. Milman.*)	32	35

Church of England (*continued*)—

	M.	E.
SS. Benet and Peter, St. Paul's Wharf (*Rev. H. C. Shuttleworth.*)	36	69
St. Catherine Coleman, Fenchurch-street (*Rt. Rev. T. E. Wilkinson.*)	84	72
St. Clement, Eastcheap (*Rev. W. J. Hall*)	98	—
St. Dunstan-in-the-East (*Rev. J. L. Ross*)	37	—
St. George, Botolph-lane (*Rev. M. McColl*)	*101	207
St. Edmund, King and Martyr, Lombard-street (*Rev. W. Benham.*)	129	203
St. James, Garlickhithe, Garlick-hill (*Rev. G. L. Gibbs*)	85	190
St. Lawrence Jewry, 34, Gresham-street (*Rev. M. Walrond.*)	97	287
St. Magnus the Martyr (*Rev. A. I. McCaul*)	70	88
St. Martin, Ludgate-hill (*Rev. Dr. J. T. White*)	20	—
St. Mary Aldermary, Bow-lane (*Rev. Dr. L. B. White*)	99	140
St. Mary-at-Hill (*Rev. A. Trower*)	47	43
St. Mary-le-Bow, Cheapside (*Rev. M. H. Vine*)	30	49
St. Mary Magdalene, Knightrider-street (*Rev. E. Hoskins.*)	52	60
St. Michael, Cornhill (*Rev. W. Hunt*)	283	362
St. Michael Bassishaw, Basinghall-street (*Rev. J. B. McCaul*)	30	23
St. Michael, Wood-street, Cheapside (*Rev. H. Hirsch*)	37	30
St. Mildred, Bread-street (*Rev. C. Engström*)	27	—
St. Nicholas, Cole Abbey (*Rev. H. C. Shuttleworth*)	124	255
St. Olave, Hart-street (*Rev. A. Povah*)	119	123
St. Olave, Old Jewry (*Rev. P. Dowe*)	14	20
St. Paul's Cathedral (*Rev. Robert Gregory*)	1662	3043
St. Peter, Cornhill (*Rev. R. Whittington*)	98	147
St. Swithin, London-stone, Cannon-street (*Rev. E. Alfree.*)	20	33
St. Vedast, Foster-lane (*Rev. Dr. W. S. Simpson*)	150	192
All Hallows, London-wall (*Rev. C. Lucy*)	47	030
St. Andrew Undershaft, Leadenhall-street (*Bishop How.*)	111	125
St. Ethelburga, Bishopsgate-street (*Rev. J. M Rodwell.*)	*111	230
St. Helen, Bishopsgate (*Rev. J. B. Deane*)	40	—
St. Katherine Cree, Leadenhall-street (*Rev. Dr. Whittemore.*)	118	92
St. Margaret, Lothbury (*Rev. A. J. Ingram*)	*150	157
St. Peter-le-Poer, Old Broad-street (*Rev. J. H. Coward.*)	60	—
St. Stephen, Coleman-street (*Rev J. W. Pratt*)	146	114

N.B.—Six important City Churches were closed on Census Sunday, so were not taken; they were—St. Bride's, Fleet-street; The Rolls Chapel; St. Margaret Patens; St. Mary Woolnoth; St. Michael, Paternoster Royal; and St. Stephen's, Walbrook.

CITY OF LONDON.

	M.	E.
Congregational—		
Bishopsgate Chapel (*Rev. T. Grear*)	*251	324
City Temple, Holborn Viaduct (*Rev. Dr. J. Parker*)	1325	2415
Ebenezer (Welsh) Church, Bartlett's-passage (*Rev. O. Evans.*)	84	274
Fetter Lane Chapel (*Vacant*)	72	67
Cannon-street Hotel (Weigh House Church) (*Rev. A. Sanderson.*)	146	130
Silver-street, Falcon-square (*Rev. A. H. Storrow*)	*308	418
Finsbury Chapel (*Rev. T. Kench*).	210	220
Independent—		
Haberdashers' Hall, Staining-lane (*Various*)	22	12
Baptist—		
Finsbury, Eldon-street (*Rev. W. Rees*)	23	88
Calvinistic Methodist—		
New Jewin Chapel, Fann-street	116	601
Moravian—		
Moravian Chapel, Fetter-lane (*Rev. J. A. Porter*).	41	19
Friends—		
Devonshire House, 12, Bishopsgate-street	41	46
French Protestant—		
French Protestant Church (*Rev. G. G. Daugars*).	67	73
Dutch Roman Catholic—		
Dutch Church, Austin Friars (*Rev. A. D. Scheltama*).	65	—
Roman Catholic—		
St. Mary, Moorfields (*Rev. Thomas F. Norris*)	310	340
St. Etheldreda, Ely-place (*Rev. William Lockhart*)	226	120
St. Peter (Italian Church) Hatton-wall (*Rev. Joseph Peter Bannin.*)	620	697
Jews—		
Synagogue, St. James-place, Aldgate (*Rev. Dr. Hermann Adler.*)	650	550
German Synagogue, New Broad Street (*Vacant*).	150	70
Hambro' Synagogue, Church Row, Fenchurch-street (*Rev. Samuel Marcus Gollanez.*)	90	90
New Synagogue, Great St. Helen's (*Rev. Isaac Cohen*)	294	387
Spanish and Portuguese Synagogue, St. Mary Axe (*Rev. David Peza.*)	165	252
Hospitals—		
St. Bartholomew-the-Less (*Rev. W. Ostle*).	175	107
Undenominational—		
Finsbury Chapel, South-place (*Dr. Andrew Wilson*).	350	—

ST. GILES-IN-THE-FIELDS.

	M.	E.
Church of England—		
Christ Church, Woburn-square (*Rev. J. J. G. Nash*)	*387	652
St. George, Hart-street (*Rev. F. F. Goe*)	477	531
Christ Church, Endell-street (*Rev. S. A. Griffiths*)	113	82
Holy Trinity, Little Queen-street (*Rev. N. Bromley*)	187	219
Seven Dials, Short's-gardens (*Rev F. S. Swindell*)	48	111
St. Giles-in-the-Fields (*Rev. J. M. Nisbet*)	269	362
West-street Episcopal Chapel (*A Lay Missionary*)	82	70
French Protestant—		
St. John, Bloomsbury-street (*Rev. A. A. Dupont*)	83	41
Baptist—		
Bloomsbury Chapel (*Rev. J. Baillie*)	686	645
Keppel Street Chapel (*Rev. W. J. Styles*)	86	108
Kingsgate Street Chapel (*Vacant*)	86	134
Little Wild Street Chapel (*Rev. G. E. Hatton*)	153	370
Wesleyan—		
Great Queen Street Chapel (*Rev. James F. Pyle*)	418	504
Swiss—		
Eglise Suisse, Endell-street (*Rev. W. Petavel*)	120	35
Roman Catholic—		
Sardinia-street, Lincoln's Inn Fields (*Rev. George S. Delaney.*)	164	319

WESTMINSTER.

	M.	E.
Church of England—		
St. James, Piccadilly (*Rev. J. E. Kempe*)	444	333
St. John the Baptist, Gt. Marlboro'-street (*Rev. H. M. D'Almaine.*)	68	98
St. Luke, Berwick-street, Soho (*Rev. A. W. Oxford*)	338	413
St. Peter, Great Windmill-street (*Rev. H. Jones*)	420	180
St. Philip, Regent-street (*Rev. H. Jones*)	133	121
St. Thomas, King-street, Regent-street. (*Rev. P. T. Bainbrigge.*)	615	500
House of Charity, Greek-street (*Rev. J. J. Elkington*)	51	33
St. Anne, Wardour-street (*Rev. N. Wade*)	386	463
St. Mary, Crown-street (*Rev. R. Gwynne*)	247	650
Congregational—		
Craven Chapel, Marshall-street, Golden-square (*Vacant*)	326	270
Wardour Chapel, Little Chapel-street (*Various*)	63	81
Baptist—		
Meard-street, Wardour-street (*Various*)	236	316

	M.	E.

Wesleyan—
Welsh Church, Poland-street (*Various*) . . 33 . 60

Welsh Calvinistic Methodist—
Nassau Street Chapel . . . . 180 . 260

Roman Catholic—
Church of the Assumption, Warwick-street . . 120 . 458
(*Hon. and Rev. Dr. Canon Talbot.*)
Notre Dame de France, 5, Leicester-place . . 280 . 360
(*Rev. Leo Thomas.*)
St. Patrick, Sutton-street, Soho-square . . 732 . 1092
(*Rev. Langton Geo. Vere.*)

Jews—
Western Synagogue, St. Alban's-place . . . 88 . *a*9
(*Rev. Hermann Davids.*)

Workhouse Chapel—
Westminster Workhouse Chapel, Poland-street . 160 . 180
(*Rev. S. H. Hayes.*)

MARYLEBONE.

Church of England—
All Saints, Margaret-street, Cavendish-square . . 417 . 513
(*Rev. W. A. Whitworth.*)
All Souls, Langham-place (*Rev. S. Douglas*) . . 768 . 931
St. Andrew, Wells-street, Oxford-street . . 808 . 1215
(*Rev. W. T. Haildsworth.*)
St. Mark, Charlotte-street (*Rev. R. Duckworth*) . . 122 . 214
St. Paul, Great Portland-street (*Rev. C. G. Williamson*) 362 . 315
St. James, Westmoreland-street (*Rev. H. R. Haweis*) . 540 . 467
St. Peter, Vere-street (*Rev. W. P. Roberts*) . . 755 . 587
Trinity Chapel, Devonshire-mews West . . No service.
(*Rev. W. Cadman.*)
Marylebone Chapel, 63, High-street . . . 168 . *a*105
(*Rev. E. G. Thomas.*)
Portman Chapel, Baker-street . . . . 1375 . 1181
(*Rev. H. N. Sherbrooke.*)
St. Marylebone, Marylebone-road (*Rev. W. Barker*) . 1292 . 1355
,,   ,,   Mission Church, Paddington-street . 71 . 165
St. Thomas, Orchard-street, Portman-square . . 371 . 302
(*Rev. H. Geary.*)
Brunswick Chapel, Upper Berkeley-street . . 296 . 321
(*Rev. E. W. Moore.*)
Quebec Chapel, 17, Old Quebec-street (*Rev. E. Bottley*) *637 . 464
St. Luke, Nutford-place (*Rev. B. H. Alford*) . . 342 . 406
St. Mark, Marylebone-road (*Rev. G. C. Bellowes*) . 200 . 140
St. Mary, Wyndham-place (*Hon. and Rev. J. Leigh*) . 296 . 351

Church of England (*continued*)—

	M.	E.
Christchurch, Stafford-street, Lisson-grove (*Rev. J. L. Davies.*)	496	309
Holy Trinity, Marylebone-road (*Rev. W. Cadman*)	450	1048
St. Barnabas, Bell-street, Edgware-road (*Rev. J. Hutchens.*)	164	280
St. Cyprian, Dorset-square (*Rev. C. Gutch*)	130	101
St. Paul, Grove-street, Lisson-grove (*Rev. E. A. Midwinter.*)	225	278
All Saints, Finchley-road (*Rev. H. S. Eyre*)	1057	674
Emmanuel Church, Aberdeen-place, Maida-hill (*Rev. J. G. Tanner.*)	549	360
St. John's Chapel, St. John's Wood-road (*Rev. H. M. Sandham.*)	228	39
St. Mark, Upper Hamilton-terrace (*Rev. Dr. R. Duckworth.*)	1106	1260
St. Matthew, Carlisle-street, Portman-market (*Rev. R. F. Spencer.*)	67	52
St. Stephen, Avenue-road, Regent's-park (*Rev. E. H. Nelson.*)	381	214

Congregational—

Paddington Chapel, Marylebone-road (*Rev. G. D. Macgregor.*)	318	316
Shouldham-st., Bryanston-square (*Rev. J. B. Warren*)	114	140
Trinity Chapel, John-street, Edgware-road (*Rev. J. O. Fellowes.*)	203	185
Greville-place Chapel, Kilburn Priory (*Rev. G. Stewart*)	120	139
St. John's Wood-terrace (*Rev. E. Griffith-Jones*)	192	214

Baptist—

Riding House-street (*Various*)	66	68
Franklin Hall, Castle-street—Welsh (*Various*)	63	181
Church-street, Edgware-road (*Rev. R. P. Cook*)	140	200
Mount Zion Church, Hill-street (*Rev. G. W. Shepherd*)	384	337
Regent's Park Chapel (*Rev. D. Davies*)	373	377
Abbey-road, St. John's Wood (*Rev. W. Stott*)	689	762
Portland-town Mission Chapel (*Various*)	97	214

Wesleyan—

Hinde-street Chapel, Manchester-square (*Rev. William J. Brown.*)	*299	285
Brunswick Chapel, Melton-street (*Rev. Albert Clayton*)	302	290
Victoria Chapel, Barrow Hill-rd. (*Rev. Sampson Weaver*)	248	222

Primitive Methodist—

Seymour-place, Bryanston-square (*Rev. W. H. Allen*)	86	78

United Methodist Free Church—

John-street West, Edgware-road (*Rev. William Horse*)	113	77

	M.	E.
Presbyterian—		
Upper George-street (*Rev. Donald Fraser*)	752	928
Marlborough-place, St. John's Wood (*Rev. J. M. Gibson*)	880	670
Unitarian—		
Little Portland-street Chapel (*Rev. P. H. Wicksteed*)	183	68
Free Episcopal—		
Carlton Hill	153	87
Roman Catholic—		
St. Charles Borromeo, Upper Ogle-st., Langham-place (*Rev. Thomas Regan.*)	584	544
The Annunciation—French Church (*Rev. Louis Toursel*)	154	49
St. James, Spanish-place (*Rev. Michael Barry*)	1100	840
Marylebone Workhouse Chapel (*Rev. A. J. Hogan*)	250	117
Our Lady of the Rosary, 209, Marylebone-road (*Rev. John J. Brenan.*)	560	469
Our Lady, Grove-road	320	430
Jews—		
Central Synagogue, Great Portland-street (*Rev. David Fay.*)	143	14
West London Synagogue (*Rev. D. W. Marks*)	81	—
Spanish Synagogue (*Rev. Joseph Peperus*)	—	20
Upper Synagogue, Marlborough-pl., St. John's Wood (*Rev. Berman Berlmer.*)	247	50
Greek Church—		
Russian Church, Welbeck-street (*Rev. Eugene Smirnoff.*)	20	—
Workhouse Chapel—		
Marylebone Workhouse Chapel (*Rev. F. Tofts*)	379	367

ST. GEORGE, HANOVER SQUARE.

Church of England—		
Hanover Church, Regent-street (*Rev. F. A. Ormsby*)	502	375
St. George, George-street, Hanover-square (*Rev. E. Capel Cure.*)	687	711
St. Mark, North Audley-street (*Rev. J. W. Ayre*)	447	349
St. Saviour, 419, Oxford-street (*Rev. C. Rhind*)	36	80
Berkeley Church, John-street (*Rev. T. T. Shore*)	315	a62
Christ Church, Down-street (*Vacant*)	377	312
Curzon Chapel, Curzon-street (*Rev. Dr. E. Ker Gray*)	151	95
Grosvenor Church, South Audley-street (*Rev. W. F. Elliott.*)	335	157
St. George's Chapel, Albemarle-street (*Rev. F. Palmer*)	16	—
St. Mary, Bourdon-street, Berkeley-square (*Rev. E. Capel Cure.*)	*410	272

Church of England (continued)—

	M.	E.
All Saints, Grosvenor-road, Pimlico (*Rev. R. Stewart*).	327	368
Eaton Church, Coleshill-street, Eaton-square (*Rev. C. A. Fox.*)	250	340
Holy Trinity, Parkside, Knightsbridge (*Rev. Dr. Wilson.*)	156	115
St. Barnabas, Church-street, Pimlico (*Rev. A. Gurney*)	382	683
St. Gabriel, Warwick-square (*Rev. J. H. J. Ellison*)	744	643
St. John (Belgrave Chapel), Belgrave-square (*Rev. A. Gurney.*)	350	—
St. John-y^e-Baptist, 50, Pimlico-road (*Rev. A. Gurney*)	315	214
St. John-y^e-Evangelist, Wilton-road (*Rev. J. Storrs*)	648	563
St. Mary, Graham-street, Pimlico (*Rev. H. M. Villiers*)	*500	660
St. Michael, Chester-square, Pimlico (*Rev. J. Fleming*)	1800	1046
St. Paul, Wilton-place, Knightsbridge (*Rev. H. M. Villiers.*)	1140	1027
St. Peter, Eaton-square, Pimlico (*Rev. J. Storrs*).	1800	1727
St. Peter's Chapel, Charlotte-street (*Rev. J. Storrs*)	499	318
St. Saviour, St. George's-square, Pimlico (*Rev. J. Walker.*)	522	781
Holy Trinity, Vauxhall-bridge-road (*Rev. G. Miller*)	313	279
St. James-the-Less, Upper Garden-street (*Rev. G. D. W. Dixon.*)	323	237
St. John the Evangelist, Smith-square (*Rev. C. W. Furse.*)	685	615
St. Mary, Vincent-square, Tothill-fields (*Rev. A. G. Warner.*)	190	247
St. Matthew, Great Peter-street (*Rev. W. B. Trevelyan*)	367	364
St. Stephen, Rochester-row (*Rev. W. M. Sinclair*)	494	411
All Saints, Ennismore-gardens, Knightsbridge (*Rev. J. Wilson.*)	501	353
Chapel Royal, Whitehall (*Rev. Edgar Sheppard*)	169	a84
Christ Church, Victoria-street (*Rev. F. K. Aglionby*)	151	342
Royal Military Church, Wellington Barracks (*Rev. R. A. Corbett.*)	714	358
St. Andrew, Ashley-place, Victoria-street (*Rev. A. G. Bowman.*)	415	1128
St. Margaret, Broad-sanctuary (*Ven. F. W. Farrar*)	1730	1362
St. Peter (Westminster Abbey) (*Rev. Dr. G. G. Bradley, Dean.*)	1721	—

Congregational—

	M.	E.
Robert-street, Grosvenor-square (*Various*)	92	80
Eccleston-square, Belgrave-road, Pimlico (*Rev. J. H. Hitchens.*)	448	427
St. Leonard-street, Vauxhall-bridge-road (*Various*)	60	56
Trevor Chapel, Trevor-square (*Vacant*)	389	337
Westminster Chapel, James-street (*Rev. H. Simon*)	535	394

	M.	*E.*
Baptist—		
Carmel Church, Westbourne-street, Pimlico (*Rev. J. Parrell.*)	71	109
Rehoboth Church, Prince's-row, Pimlico (*Rev. J. Hand*)	80	103
Romney-street Chapel, Westminster (*Rev. G. Davies*).	202	225
Wesleyan—		
Claverton-street, Pimlico (*Rev. Benjamin Broadley*)	258	332
Horseferry-road (*Rev. Thos. E. Brigden*)	430	671
United Methodist Free Church—		
Pimlico Chapel, Westmoreland-street (*Rev. C. Tregoning.*)	119	110
Victoria Chapel, Vauxhall-bridge-road (*Rev. J. Hocking*)	131	168
Presbyterian—		
Halkin-street West, Belgrave-square (*Rev. A. Saphir*)	264	137
Catholic Apostolic—		
Orchard-street, Victoria-street (*Various*)	39	27
Roman Catholic—		
Immaculate Conception, Farm-street, Berkeley-square (*Rev. Edward Purbrick.*)	323	—
St. Mary, Horseferry-road (*Rev. Francis Scoles*)	377	651
SS. Peter and Edward, Palace-street, Pimlico (*Rev. Cyril W. Forster.*)	312	320
Hospital Chapel—		
Emanuel Hospital Chapel (*Rev. J. Maskell*)	22	—
St. George's Hospital, Grosvenor-place	115	40

HOLBORN.

INCLUDING HOLBORN AND PORTIONS OF CLERKENWELL, PENTONVILLE, AND CITY ROAD.

	M.	*E.*
Church of England—		
Lincoln's Inn Chapel, Lincoln's Inn (*Rev. Dr. H. Wace.*)	Closed	
Gray's Inn Chapel, Gray's Inn-square (*Rev. Dr. T. H. Stokoe.*)	74	—
St. George-the-Martyr, Queen's-square (*Rev. D. Craven.*)	410	320
St. John-the-Evangelist, Red Lion-square (*Rev. E. C. Coney.*)	203	312
St. Alban-the-Martyr, Brook-street (*Rev. A. J. Suckling*)	767	533
Charterhouse Church (*Rev. R. Elwyn*)	68	—
St. Peter, Great Saffron-hill (*Rev. E. Canney*)	81	186
St. James, Clerkenwell-green (*Rev. J. H. Rose*)	360	325
St. John the Baptist, St. John's-square (*Rev. W. Dawson.*)	67	144

Church of England (*continued*)—

	M.	E.
St. Philip, Granville-square, King's Cross-road (*Rev. J. S. Jones.*)	246	269
St. James, Pentonville-road (*Rev. S. D. Stubbs*)	101	102
St. Silas, Penton-street (*Rev. E. G. Hall*)	191	222
St. Stephen Mission Church, White Lion-street (*Rev. J. Cross.*)	63	113
St. Mark, Middleton-square (*Rev. R. L. Giveen*)	379	501
St. Peter, St. John-street-road (*Rev. B. O. Sharp*)	209	256
St. Barnabas, King's-square (*Rev. R. Heyliger*)	51	72
St. Matthew, City-road (*Rev. G. H. Perry*)	510	370
St. Paul, Peartree-street (*Rev. A. S. Herring*)	289	155
St. Clement, Lever-street (*Rev. J. Longridge*)	189	234
St. Luke, Old-street (*Rev. W. G. Abbott*)	*807	559
St. Mary, Charterhouse, Playhouse-yard (*Rev. N. Dawes.*)	183	346
St. Paul, Bunhill-row (*Rev. G. Smith*)	135	159

Congregational—

	M.	E.
Claremont Chapel (*Rev. W. Whitley*)	158	267
Pentonville-road Chapel, King's Cross (*Rev. Bevil Allen.*)	152	227
City-road Chapel (*Rev. G. Thompson*)	*255	310
Whitefield Tabernacle, Tabernacle-walk (*Rev. J. Morgan.*)	334	641

Independent—

	M.	E.
Woodbridge-street Chapel (*Rev. George Davis*)	99	97
Providence Chapel, Regent-street, City-road (*Rev. William Sinden.*)	115	110

Baptist—

	M.	E.
John-street Chapel (*Rev. J. E. Shephard*)	136	291
Clerkenwell-road (*Various*)	45	43
Vernon Chapel, Vernon-square (*Rev. C. B. Sawday*)	*333	700
Chadwell-street, Clerkenwell (*Rev. J. Hazelton*)	248	322
Charles-street, City-road (*Rev. Philip Gast*)	114	249
James'-street Chapel, St. Luke's (*Rev. E. J. Farley*)	40	86
Great Arthur-street	620	234

Wesleyan—

	M.	E.
St. John's-square (*Rev. Edward Smith*)	205	370
City-road Chapel (*Rev. John M'Kenny*)	*685	536
Welsh Chapel, City-road (*Rev. John Hughes*)	68	277

Friends—

	M.	E.
Peel-court, Smithfield (*Various*)	32	22

Lady Huntingdon's Connexion—

	M.	E.
Spa-fields Chapel (*Rev. E. J. Bird*)	175	331

	M.	E.
Roman Catholic—		
SS. Peter and Paul, Rosoman-street	185	313
(Rev. Joseph L. Biemans.)		
St. Joseph, Lamb's-buildings, Bunhill-row	290	172
(Rev. David Toomey.)		

STRAND.

	M.	E.
Church of England—		
Chapel Royal, St. James's Palace	Closed	
(Rev. Edgar Sheppard.)		
St. John, Broad-court, Drury-lane (Rev. E. Venables)	202	310
St. Martin-in-the-Fields, Trafalgar-square	548	576
(Rev. J. Fenwick Kitto.)		
Chapel Royal, Savoy, Victoria Embankment	Closed	
(Rev. H. White.)		
King's College Chapel, 160, Strand (Rev. Dr. Wace)	58	—
St. Mary-le-Strand (Rev. L. Tugwell)	84	84
St. Paul, Covent-garden (Rev. S. Cumberlege)	125	194
St. Clement Danes, Strand (Rev. J. Lindsay)	212	353
Congregational—		
Orange-street Chapel (Various)	73	82
Presbyterian—		
Whitfield Chapel (Rev. B. Alexander)	46	67
Church of Scotland—		
Crown-court, Drury-lane (Rev. H. M. Philip)	155	135
German Lutheran—		
German Chapel Royal, St. James' Palace	101	—
(Rev. Dr. Walbaum.)		
Roman Catholic—		
Corpus Christi, Maiden-lane (Rev. Philip Phillips)	225	252
Jews—		
Maiden-lane Synagogue	31	24

CAMBERWELL.

Comprising the Sub-Districts of Dulwich, Camberwell, and Peckham.

	M.	E.
Church of England—		
Chapel of Alleyne's College, Dulwich	476	359
(Rev. G. W. Daniell.)		
Dulwich College Chapel of Ease (Rev. G. W. Daniell)	287	111
St. Paul, Herne-hill (Rev. G. S. Bridge)	499	328
St. Stephen, Dulwich (Rev. M. A. Clark)	397	209
Camden Church, Peckham-road	558	481
(Ven. Archd. Richardson.)		

Church of England (continued):—

	M.	E.
Emmanuel Church, Dulwich (*Rev. B. Forster*)	*300	460
St. Clement, Dulwich (*Rev. H. E. Jennings*)	667	700
St. Giles, Church-street (*Rev. F. Kelly*)	1020	962
St. James, Knatchbull-road (*Rev. J. D. Dyke*)	*621	798
St. John, East Dulwich (*Rev. T. A. Warburton*)	1090	860
St. Peter, Dulwich (*Rev. W. Calvert*)	589	434
St. Saviour, Denmark-park (*Rev. H. S. Swithenbank*)	767	851
All Saints, Blenheim-grove (*Rev. J. Gaster*)	*562	518
Christ Church, Old Kent-road (*Rev. R. O. T. Thorpe*)	364	367
Licensed Victuallers' Asylum	*238	449
St. Andrew, Glengale-road (*Rev. W. S. Cadman*)	151	249
St. Antholin, Nunhead (*Rev. A. Drew*)	671	900
St. Chrysostom, Hill-street (*Rev. J. Haycroft*)	272	302
St. Jude, Meeting House-lane (*Rev. C. J. Meade*)	675	625
St. Mary Magdalene (*Rev. T. Smith*)	785	994
St. George, Well-street (*Rev. N. Campbell*)	345	521
St. Luke, Rosemary-road (*Rev. H. B. Chapman*)	574	1104
St. Philip, Old Kent-road (*Rev. T. H. L. Leary*)	205	327
St. Mark, Old Kent-road (*Rev. A. R. Goodacre*)	156	177
St. Dunstan, East Dulwich (*Rev. W. Calvert*)	227	111
St. Mark, Peckham (*Rev. G. Collett*)	521	331

Congregational—

	M.	E.
Camberwell-green (*Rev. C. Clemance*)	490	376
Camberwell New-road, Charles-street (*Rev. W. Tubb*)	*220	142
Dulwich-grove (*Rev. D. Alexander*)	194	216
Clifton Chapel, Peckham (*Rev. H. J. Perkins*)	491	756
Hanover Chapel, Peckham (*Rev. G. B. Ryley*)	440	507
Linden-grove, Peckham (*Rev. J. C. Postans*)	443	292
Albany-road (*Rev. J. B. French*)	156	152
Marlborough Chapel, Old Kent-road (*Rev. H. E. Arkell.*)	484	562

Independent—

	M.	E.
Grove Independent Chapel, Camberwell (*Rev. T. Bradbury.*)	374	343

Baptist—

	M.	E.
Mansion House, Camberwell (*Rev. G. W. Linnecur*)	*236	545
John's-street, Camberwell (*Various*)	29	57
Lordship-lane (*Rev. T. Perry*)	296	412
Wyndham-road, Camberwell (*Rev. J. Creer*)	*297	454
Barry-road, East Dulwich (*Rev. A. J. Grant*)	116	102
South London Tabernacle (*Vacant*)	350	311
Peckham Public Hall (*Various*)	74	107
Park-road, Peckham (*Rev. H. O. Mackey*)	355	542
Rye-lane, Peckham (*Rev. J. T. Briscoe*)	*1131	1354
Lausanne-road, Hatcham (*Rev. J. T. Cole*)	290	194
Heaton-road, Peckham (*Various*)	126	108

	M.	E.
Baptist (*continued*)—		
Cottage-green, Southampton-street (*Rev. J. A. Brown*)	182	203
James-grove, Peckham (*Rev. J. E. Bennett*)	160	245
Maze Pond Chapel, Old Kent-road (*Rev. W. P. Cope*)	289	688
Gordon-road, Peckham (*Rev. T. H. Court*)	*221	247
Nunhead-green (*Rev. J. Mead*)	177	165
Wesleyan—		
Barry-road, Peckham Rye (*Rev. Anthony Ward*)	748	705
Queen's-road, Peckham (*Rev. Samuel T. House*)	722	648
Oakley-place, Old Kent-road (*Rev. T. W. Johnstone*)	360	441
Tustin Chapel, Old Kent-road (*Rev. F. C. Stuart*)	*236	280
Primitive Methodist—		
Sumner-road, Peckham (*Rev. James W. Coad*)	63	64
United Methodist Free Church—		
Hill-street, Peckham (*Rev. H. Codling*)	115	184
Bellenden-road, Peckham (*Rev R. Abercrombie*)	98	157
Methodist New Connexion—		
Zion Chapel, Neat-street, Albany-road. (*Rev. Wm. W. Howard*)	88	111
Presbyterian—		
Brunswick-square, Denmark-hill (*Rev. J. R. Howatt*)	459	376
Church of Scotland—		
East Dulwich-road (*Rev. N. Stewart*)	244	193
Friends—		
Meeting House, Hanover-street (*Various*)	128	73
German Evangelical—		
Windsor-road, Denmark-hill (*Rev. A. Hysard*)	97	—
New Jerusalem Church—		
Pelican Hall, Peckham-road (*Rev. W. C. Barlow*)	25	29
Flodden-road, Camberwell (*Rev. R. J. Tilson*)	*108	137
Unitarian—		
East Surrey-grove	62	51
Avondale-road, Peckham (*Rev. J. S. Mummery*)	101	83
Christadelphian—		
Camberwell New-road (*Various*)	—	33
Roman Catholic—		
St. Anthony, Lordship-lane (*Rev. F. Joseph*)	183	138
Our Lady, Lower Park-road (*Rev. F. Liborius*)	292	435
Workhouses and Hospitals—		
Camberwell Workhouse, Havil-street (*Rev. G. W. B. Arnold*)	102	88
Camberwell Workhouse, Gordon-road (*Rev. G. W. B. Arnold*)	342	252

LAMBETH.

Comprising the Sub-Districts of Waterloo-road, Lambeth, Kennington, Brixton, and Norwood.

Church of England—

	M.	E.
St. Andrew, Lambeth (*Rev. T. M. Fielder*)	139	242
St. John, Waterloo-road (*Rev. A. Jephson*)	253	550
All Saints, York-street (*Rev. Dr. Lee*)	41	66
St. Thomas, Westminster Bridge-road (*Rev. J. Starey*)	240	181
Holy Trinity, Lambeth (*Rev. W. Warren*)	185	236
St. Mary, Lambeth-road (*Hon. and Rev. F. G. Pelham*)	*916	498
Emmanuel Church, Lambeth (*Rev. E. M. Walker*)	240	332
St. Mary, Princes-road (*Rev. G. H. Bromfield*)	552	289
St. Peter, Upper Kennington-lane (*Rev. G. W. Herbert*)	*197	600
St. Philip, Kennington-road (*Rev. J. H. Walshew*)	123	220
All Saints, South Lambeth (*Rev. A. T. Edwards*)	1030	820
St. Anne, Lambeth-road South (*Rev. W. A. Harrison*)	*370	590
St. Barnabas, Guildford-road (*Rev. W. W. Edwards*)	337	452
St. James, Kennington Park-road (*Rev. S. B. Harris*)	139	249
St. Silas, Dawlish-street (*Rev. W. W. Edwards*)	126	170
St. Stephen, South Lambeth (*Rev. J. S. Pratt*)	*526	578
St. Augustine, Clapham-rise (*Rev. A. Edwards*)	373	465
Christ Church, Brixton-road North (*Rev. J. Hussey*)	786	991
St. Andrew, Stockwell-green (*Rev. C. E. Escreet*)	464	605
St. John, Vassall-road, Kennington (*Rev. C. E. Brooke*)	817	938
St. Mark, Kennington (*Rev. H. Montgomery*)	815	1093
St. Michael, Stockwell (*Rev. M. H. Begbie*)	421	660
St. Catherine, Loughboro'-park (*Rev. J. Row*)	167	185
St. John, Angell Town (*Rev. C. J. R. Cooke*)	501	396
St. Jude, Herne-hill (*Rev. R. B. Ransford*)	759	1117
St. Matthew, Brixton (*Rev. N. A. Garland*)	1002	729
St. Matthew, Denmark-hill (*Rev. S. Carolin*)	515	560
St. Paul, West Brixton (*Rev. G. V. Concanon*)	940	998
St. Saviour, Herne-hill-road (*Rev. L. T. Chavasse*)	534	584
St. Saviour, Lambert-road (*Rev. F. G. Sanders*)	532	400
St. Matthias, Upper Tulse-hill (*Rev. W. C. Moore*)	313	260
Christ Church, Gipsy-hill (*Rev. R. Allen*)	915	643
Emmanuel Church, West Dulwich (*Rev. E. Rae*)	*556	742
Holy Trinity, Tulse-hill (*Rev. W. C. Moore*)	708	754
St. John, Upper Norwood (*Rev. W. F. Bateman*)	882	561
St. Luke, Lower Norwood (*Rev. J. Gilmore*)	500	402

Congregational—

	M.	E.
Claylands Chapel, Clapham-road (*Rev. J. Foster*)	184	183
Priory Chapel, Wandsworth-road (*Rev. J. Le Pla*)	*225	293
Brixton Independent Church (*Rev. Dr. Stevenson*)	810	1276
Loughboro' Park Chapel (*Rev. D. A. Herschell*)	399	355
Stockwell-road (*Rev. C. Chambers*)	396	191

LAMBETH. 15

	M.	E.
Congregational *(continued)*—		
Trinity Church, Brixton (*Rev. W. Herbert*)	313	219
York-road Chapel (*Rev. T. Davies*)	385	307
Dulwich Church, Park-road (*Rev. A. C. Tarbolton*)	127	80
Christ Church, Westminster-bridge-road (*Rev. Newman Hall.*)	818	1296
Lower Norwood, Chapel-road (*Rev. S. King*)	275	243
Esher-street, Kennington-lane (*Vacant*)	106	175
Baptist—		
Stockwell Baptist Chapel (*Vacant*)	772	943
Providence Chapel, Auckland-hill (*Various*)	79	59
Brixton Tabernacle, Stockwell-road (*Rev. C. Cornwell*)	188	203
Cornwall-road, Brixton (*Rev. E. P. Barrett*)	*161	406
Denmark-place (*Rev. S. B. Rees*)	482	400
Gresham Chapel, Barrington-road (*Rev. J. T. Swift*)	386	448
Solon-road, Brixton (*Rev. J. Douglas*)	358	370
Metropolitan Tabernacle (*Rev. C. H. Spurgeon*)	4519	6070
Regent-street Chapel, Lambeth (*Rev. T. C. Page*)	135	167
Wynne-road, Brixton (*Rev. J. C. Brown*)	152	85
Charles-street, Camberwell New-road (*Rev. J. A. Griffin.*)	301	344
Gipsy-road, Lower Norwood (*Rev. W. Hobbs*)	365	423
Vauxhall Chapel, Kennington-lane (*Rev. T. J. Malyon*)	155	284
Chatsworth-road, Lower Norwood (*Rev. W. F. Gooch*)	424	584
Bedford-row, Clapham (*Rev. W. Tooke*)	47	56
Wesleyan—		
John-street, South Lambeth (*Rev. Richard Roberts*)	32	43
Studley-road, Stockwell (*Rev. William Waters*)	526	485
Vauxhall-walk (*Rev. W. Wood*)	182	189
Mostyn-road, Kennington (*Rev. John Walton*)	425	413
Knight's-hill, Norwood (*Rev. W. H. Thompson*)	180	167
Brixton-hill (*Rev. F. J. Sharr*)	660	1030
Roupell-park (*Rev. T. H. Hopkins*)	485	364
Lambeth-road (*Rev. Richard Roberts*)	471	583
Westow-hill, Upper Norwood (*Rev. R. J. Meyer*)	613	857
United Methodist Free Church—		
Miles Street, Vauxhall (*Rev. J. Roberts*)	230	185
Railton-road, Herne-hill (*Rev. J. Hocking*)	293	244
Paradise-road, Stockwell (*Rev. H. Codling*)	81	82
Methodist New Connexion—		
Southwell Chapel, Wandsworth-road (*Rev. Dr. C. D. Ward.*)	55	56

Primitive Methodist—   M.   E.
  Thomas-street, Kennington-park (*Rev. F. R. Andrews*)   85   125
  Hamilton-road, Norwood (*Rev. William Wray*)   71   82
  Windsor-road, Lower Norwood (*Rev. William Wray*)   21   24
Presbyterian—
  Verulam Church, Kennington-road (*Rev. P. A. Milne*)   123   188
  Trinity Church, Clapham-road (*Rev. Dr. MacEwan*)   736   421
Catholic Apostolic—
  Camberwell New-road (*Rev. W. Hackery*)   285   198
Unitarian—
  Effra-road, Brixton (*Rev. W. M. Ainsworth*)   128   55
Free Church—
  Immanuel Church, Brixton (*Rev. Aubrey Price*)   247   236
Bible Christian —
  Waterloo-road (*Rev. W. H. Pickell*)   191   250
Christadelphian—
  Westminster Bridge-road   —   96
Roman Catholic—
  Camberwell New-road (*Rev. Jos. C. C. McGrath*)   620   700
  Convent, Norwood (*Rev. Francis O'Callaghan*)   273   186
Hospital, Workhouse, etc.—
  St. Thomas's Hospital (*Rev. J. Grant Mills*)   82   —
  Lambeth Workhouse (*Rev. W. H. Langworthy*)   500   —
  Norwood Industrial School (*Rev. W. H. Seffins*)   491   497

ST. SAVIOUR, SOUTHWARK.

Comprising Sub-Districts of Christ Church; St. Saviour, Kent Road; Borough Road; London Road; Trinity, Newington; St. Mary, Newington; St. Peter, Walworth.

Church of England—
  Christ Church, Blackfriars-road (*Rev. A. H. de Fontaine*)   263   509
  All Hallows, Pepper-street, Union-street   194   186
    (*Rev. G. W. Berkeley.*)
  St. Peter, Sumner-street (*Vacant*)   101   116
  St. Saviour, Borough High-street (*Rev. W. Thompson*)   687   391
  St. George-the-Martyr, High-street (*Rev. B. Cassin*)   408   815
  St. Stephen, Tabard-street (*Rev. W. Dodge*)   93   127
  St. Alphege, Lancaster-street (*Rev. A. B. Goulden*)   312   517
  St. Michael, Lant-street (*Rev. Dr. Newton*)   37   37
  St. Jude, St. George's-road (*Rev. J. W. Pitchford*)   170   265
  St. Paul, Westminster Bridge-road (*Rev. E. N. Willson*)   Closed.
  Holy Trinity, Trinity-square (*Rev. D. A. Moullin*)   210   137
  St. Andrew, New Kent-road (*Rev. L. S. E. Trousdale*)   312   517

ST. SAVIOUR, SOUTHWARK.

	M.	E.
Church of England (*continued*)—		
St. Matthew, New Kent-road (*Rev. J. M. Cadman*)	281	153
All Saints, Surrey-square (*Rev. O. Mitchell*)	*474	929
All Souls, Grosvenor-park (*Rev. Dr. Hill*)	178	133
St. Mark, Walworth (*Rev. W. E. Evill*)	138	264
St. Peter, Beckford-row (*Rev. N. M. Mungeam*)	361	506
St. Stephen, Walworth-common (*Rev. G. A. Ormsby*)	434	540
St. Agnes, Kennington (*Rev. T. B. Dover*)	492	390
St. Gabriel, Newington	227	264
St. John, York-street (*Rev. G. T. Cotham*)	141	170
St. Mary, Kennington Park-road (*Rev. G. T. Palmer*)	384	788
St. Paul, Lorrimore-square (*Rev. E. F. Alexander*)	476	527
St. Mary Magdalene, Clarence-street (*Rev. Henry Watts.*)	251	154
Congregational—		
Pilgrim Church, New Kent-road (*Rev. F. Barclay*)	205	424
Borough-road Chapel (*Rev. G. M. Murphy*)	208	281
Southwark Bridge-road (Welsh) (*Rev. F. Thomas*)	57	172
Sutherland Chapel, Walworth (*Rev. C. Chandler*)	126	225
York-street, Walworth (*Rev. J. P. Turquand*)	109	224
Collier's Rents, New Kent-road (*Rev. Dr. Wilson*)	52	62
Baptist—		
Borough-road (*Rev. G. W. McCree*)	122	223
Upton Chapel, Burkham-terrace (*Rev. W. Williams*)	851	879
Arthur-street, Camberwell-gate (*Rev. S. H. Akehurst*)	210	247
East-street, Walworth-road (*Rev. T. A. Carver*)	204	201
York-street, Walworth-road (*Various*)	7	10
Surrey Tabernacle (*Vacant*)	616	749
Walworth-road (*Rev. W. J. Mills*)	357	455
Wesleyan—		
Stamford-street (*Rev. Richard Roberts*)	109	149
Lock's Fields, Rodney-road (*Rev. W. R. Stewart*)	223	164
Camberwell-road, Walworth (*Rev. J. Hugh Morgan*)	338	651
Methodist New Connexion—		
Brunswick Church, Great Dover-road (*Rev. Wm. W. Howard*)	134	229
Kingslake-street, Old Kent-road (*Rev. Wm. W. Howard*)	115	109
Primitive Methodist—		
Surrey Chapel, Blackfriars-rd. (*Rev. Benjamin Senior*)	108	147
Trinity-street, Borough (*Rev. Frederic R. Andrews*)	82	63
East-street, Walworth-road (*Rev. James W. Coad*)	57	145
Presbyterian—		
St. George, Borough-road (*Rev. H. M. Mackenzie*)	129	126

		M.	E.
Unitarian—			
Stamford-street Chapel (*Rev. C. Bowie*)		79	136
Peculiar People—			
Bath-street, London-road (*Various*)		33	32
Christians—			
Beresford-street (*Various*)		325	336
Roman Catholic—			
St. George's Church, St. George's-road		2273	2634
(*Canon Wm. Murnane.*)			
Jews—			
Vowler-street, Walworth-road (*Rev. F. L. Cohen*)		55	14

ST. OLAVE, SOUTHWARK.

Comprising the Sub-Districts of St. Olave; Leather Market; St. Mary Magdalene; St. James, Bermondsey; Rotherhithe.

	M.	E.
Church of England—		
St. John, Horselydown (*Rev. W. J. Batchelor*)	*266	443
St. Olave, Tooley-street (*Rev. Dr. Maguire*)	126	178
St. Thomas, St. Thomas-street (*Rev. O. Robinson*)	56	—
St. Paul, Nelson-street, Bermondsey	132	103
(*Rev. S. M. Mayhew.*)		
St. Mary, Bermondsey (*Rev. C. d'A. Lawrence*)	292	466
Christ Church, Dockhead (*Rev. W. L. Bell*)	88	297
St. Anne, Thorburn-square, Bermondsey	*360	652
(*Rev. J. B. Walsh.*)		
St. Augustine, Lynton-road (*Rev. J. Stobart*)	357	405
St. Crispin, Jamaica-level (*Rev. W. Powell*)	152	96
St. James, Bermondsey (*Rev. W. Allan*)	354	440
All Saints, Deptford Lower-road (*Rev. W. West*)	111	153
Christ Church, Rotherhithe (*Rev. H. C. Michenson*)	214	335
Holy Trinity, Rotherhithe (*Rev. J. Wilson*)	122	121
St. Mary, Rotherhithe (*Rev. J. E. Beck*)	247	117
St. Barnabas, Rotherhithe (*Rev. R. Russell*)	136	118
St. Luke, Bermondsey (*Rev. F. J. Hensley*)	213	302
Congregational—		
Union Chapel, Horselydown (*Rev. J. S. T. Smith*)	205	181
Jamaica-row, Bermondsey (*Rev. J. Farren*)	268	268
Rouel-road, Bermondsey (*Rev. G. McAll*)	139	293
Maynard-road, Rotherhithe (*Rev. J. Holway*)	84	71
Southwark Park (*Rev. F. A. Billing*)	159	144
Baptist—		
Drummond-road, Bermondsey (*Rev. B. Brigg*)	246	354
Lynton-road, Grange-road (*Rev. William Ward*)	132	101

	M.	E.
Baptist (*continued*)—		
New Church-street (*Rev. J. L. Meeres*)	158	140
Abbey-street (*Rev. J. Carlile*)	179	203
Rotherhithe New-road (*Vacant*)	172	203
Wesleyan—		
Silver-street, Rotherhithe (*Rev. T. W. Johnstone*)	104	101
Southwark Park (*Rev. W. R. Stewart*)	*530	810
Southwark Chapel, Chapel-place (*Rev. T. W. Johnstone*)	*390	940
United Methodist Free Church—		
Grange-road, Bermondsey (*Rev. H. Codling*)	105	130
Manor Chapel, Bermondsey (*Rev. W. Dunstan*)	197	327
Albion-street, Rotherhithe (*Rev. W. Mildon*)	145	109
Union-road, Rotherhithe (*Rev. H. Codling*)	70	100
St. James Hall, St. James-road (*Rev. W. Mildon*)	80	55
Welsh Calvinistic Methodist—		
Crosby-row, King-street, Borough	73	238
Presbyterian—		
Southwark Park-road (*Rev. Thomas Curry*)	75	160
Nor. Lutheran—		
Ebenezer, Derrick-street (*Rev. S. H. Jensen*)	293	75
Roman Catholic—		
Our Lady, Trinity-street (*Rev. Charles Kimpé*)	60	20
Most Holy Trinity, Dockhead (*Rev. Charles Huggett*)	325	621
Our Lady, Melior-street	152	239
Hospital—		
Guy's Hospital, Southwark	126	86

SHOREDITCH.

COMPRISING THE SUB-DISTRICTS OF HOLYWELL; ST. LEONARD; HOXTON NEW TOWN; HOXTON OLD TOWN; HAGGERSTON.

Church of England—		
St. Agatha, Wilson-street, Finsbury-square (*Rev. F. C. Wills.*)	77	133
St. James, Curtain-road (*Rev. A. J. Buss*)	232	164
St. Leonard, Shoreditch (*Rev. S. Buss*)	285	475
St. Michael, Mark-street, Finsbury (*Rev. H. D. Nihill*)	159	103
Holy Trinity, Hoxton (*Rev. W. H. Sotheby*)	103	400
St. Mark, Old-street (*Rev. T. C. Webster*)	108	110
St. Mary, Hoxton (*Rev. N. J. Devereux*)	181	334
Christ Church, New North-road (*Rev. H. P. Kelly*)	83	187
St. Anne, Hoxton-street (*Rev. W. M. Pullock*)	79	120
St. John, New North-road (*Rev. G. P. Pownall*)	403	701
St. Peter, Hoxton-square (*Rev. T. Priestly*)	51	111
St. Saviour, Hyde-road (*Rev. W. W. Goddard*)	339	619

	M.	E.
Church of England (*continued*)—		
All Saints, Haggerston (*Rev. W. St. H. Bourne*)	252	301
St. Andrew, Hoxton (*Rev. H. Hayman*)	83	125
St. Augustine, Haggerston (*Rev. J. N. Burrows*)	403	355
St. Chad, Haggerston (*Rev. W. R. Sharpe*)	400	234
St. Columba, Haggerston (*Rev. J. V. Walters*)	132	111
St. Mary, Haggerston (*Rev. A. Tanner*)	345	362
St. Paul, Haggerston (*Rev. S. J. Stone*)	336	423
St. Stephen, Haggerston (*Rev. G. Morris*)	116	127
Congregational—		
Pownall-road, Dalston (*Rev. R. Mackay*)	150	165
Barbican Chapel, New North-road (*Rev. J. Boyle*)	240	350
New Tabernacle, Old-street (*Rev. Peter H. Davies*)	143	387
Baptist—		
Queen's-road, Dalston (*Rev. W. Miall*)	62	78
Bethel Church, Hoxton (*Various*)	45	34
Jireh Chapel, East-road (*Rev. W. Waite*)	20	30
Wesleyan—		
Hertford-street, Haggerston (*Rev. R. P. Downes*)	84	107
New North-road, Hoxton (*Rev. J. R. Berry*)	262	318
United Methodist Free Church—		
Maidstone-street, Haggerston (*Rev. Thomas Foster*)	50	53
Willow-street, Shoreditch (*Rev. W. Treyall*)	110	170
Primitive Methodist—		
Philip-street, Hoxton (*Rev. John Hammond*)	61	107
Bible Christians—		
Jubilee Chapel, East-road (*Rev. W. Jeffery*)	150	130
Believers—		
Westmoreland-place, City-road (*Various*)	51	47
Roman Catholic—		
St. Monica, Hoxton-square (*Rev. Dr. Michael Kelly*)	132	194
Workhouse—		
St. Luke's Workhouse, Shepherdess-walk (*Rev. A. P. Hockin.*)	160	120

BETHNAL-GREEN.

COMPRISING THE SUB-DISTRICTS OF HACKNEY ROAD, BETHNAL GREEN, BETHNAL GREEN CHURCH, AND BETHNAL GREEN TOWN.

	M.	E.
Church of England—		
St. Simon Zelotes, Bethnal-green (*Rev. E. P. Green*)	109	159
St. John, Cambridge-road (*Rev. H. B. Bromby*)	536	625
St. James-the-Less, Victoria-park (*Rev. G. Moon*)	282	298

WHITECHAPEL.

	M.	E.
Church of England (*continued*)—		
St. Bartholomew, Essex-street (*Rev. J. Clemmens*)	120	155
St. Barnabas, Grove-road (*Rev. G. Barnes*)	123	188
St. Philip, Friars-mount (*Rev. R. R. W. Loveridge*)	121	245
St. Matthias, Hare-street (*Rev. F. W. Briggs*)	103	317
St. Matthew, Church-row (*Rev. S. C. H. Hansard*)	*378	896
Holy Trinity, Church-street, Shoreditch (*Rev. W. Shakespear.*)	41	50
St. Paul, Bethnal Green (*Rev. B. Grant*)	34	105
St. Jude, Bethnal Green (*Rev. Alfred Strugnell*)	175	197
St. James-the-Great (*Rev. E. F. Coke*)	55	56
St. Andrew, Viaduct-street (*Hon. and Rev. F. Adderley*)	144	242
St. Peter, Hackney-road (*Rev. T. Woolley*)	286	284
St. Thomas, Baroness-road (*Rev. H. Fawcett*)	140	220
Jews' Episcopal Chapel (*Rev. J. B. Barraclough*)	378	277
Congregational—		
Adelphi Chapel, Hackney-road (*Rev. R. B. Lander*)	271	570
Bethnal Green-road (*Rev. J. S. Watts*)	323	567
Approach-road, Victoria Park (*Rev. Thomas Evans*)	*885	953
Sydney-street (*Rev. T. J. R. Temple*)	162	187
Baptist—		
Grove-road, Victoria-park (*Rev. W. J. Inglis*)	403	433
Hope Chapel, Norton-street (*Rev. J. Copeland*)	122	105
Bethnal Green-road (*Rev. W. H. Smith*)	188	282
Shalom Chapel, The Oval (*Rev. H. Myerson*)	77	86
Shoreditch Tabernacle (*Rev. W. Cuff*)	1033	1468
Wesleyan—		
Hackney-road (*Rev. J. R. Berry*)	232	383
Approach-road, Victoria Park (*Rev. Thos. T. Lambert*)	479	532
Primitive Methodist—		
Memorial Church, The Oval (*Rev. G. Shapcott*)	85	99

WHITECHAPEL.

COMPRISING THE SUB-DISTRICTS OF SPITALFIELDS, MILE-END NEW TOWN, WHITECHAPEL CHURCH, GOODMAN'S-FIELDS, AND ALDGATE.

	M.	E.
Church of England—		
St. Mark, Whitechapel (*Rev. G. Davenport*)	246	180
St. Paul, Dock-street (*Rev. D. Greatorex*)	187	219
Holy Trinity, Minories (*Rev. E. M. Tomlinson*)	22	57
St. Mary Matfelon, Whitechapel-road (*Rev. A. J. Robinson.*)	531	591
St. Peter-ad-Vincula, Tower (*Rev. F. J. Rogers*)	230	103
St. Jude, Commercial-street (*Rev. S. A. Barnett*)	96	154
Christ Church, Commercial-street (*Rev. R. C. Billing*)	191	338
St. Mary, Spital-square (*Rev. M. Thomas*)	171	116

Church of England (*continued*)—	M.	E.
St. Stephen, Commercial-street . .	144	175
(*Rev. J. S. Whichelow.*)	
All Saints, Mile-end New Town (*Rev. H. A. Mason*) .	120	222
St. Olave, Mile-end New Town (*Rev. E. L. Green*) .	*79	204

Congregational—
Trinity Church, Mile-end New Town . . | *156 | 189
(*Rev. Dr. W. Tyler.*) | |
Sion Chapel, Whitechapel-road (*Rev. A. W. Bennett*). | 101 | 147

Baptist—
Artillery-street, Spitalfields (*Various*) . . | 41 | 53
Little Alie-street (*Rev. R. E. Sears*) . . | 141 | 113
Commercial-street, Whitechapel (*Rev. W. T. Adey*) . | 63 | 59
Zoar Chapel, Great Alie-street (*Rev. E. Ashdown*) . | 243 | 237

Wesleyan—
Church-street, Spitalfields (*Rev. William Johnson*) . | 86 | 109

United Methodist Free Church—
Hanbury-street, Spitalfields (*Rev. Thomas Foster*) | 28 | 49

Friends—
Bedford Institute, Wheeler-street . . | 67 | 76

Lutheran—
St. George, Little Alie-street (*Rev. Dr. Cappel*) . | 102 | 83

Roman Catholic—
English Martyrs, Great Prescot-street . . | 510 | 500
(*Rev. W. M. J. Ring.*) | |
St. Ann, Albert-place . . . . . | 629 | 380

Hospital Church—
London Hospital, Whitechapel (*Rev. H. T. Valentine*) | 146 | 127

ST. GEORGE-IN-THE-EAST.

COMPRISING THE SUB-DISTRICTS OF ST. GEORGE (NORTH), AND ST. JOHN.

Church of England—
St. Peter, Old Gravel-lane (*Rev. L. S. Wainwright*) .	226	220
St. Matthew, Princes-square (*Rev. J. M. Fidler*) .	131	207
St. Mary, Johnston-street (*Rev. H. Sinden*) . .	48	82
St. John the Evangelist (*Rev C. T. C. Bennett*) .	98	128
St. George-in-the-East (*Rev. C. H. Turner*) . .	292	425
Christ Church, Watney-street (*Rev. W. P. Jay*) .	234	254

Congregational—
Ebenezer Chapel, Watney-street (*Rev. B. Sackett*) | 137 | 335

	M.	E.
Baptist—		
Commercial-road (*Rev. J. Fletcher*)	320	376
Wesleyan—		
Dee-street (*Rev. William Hirst*)	144	64
St. George's Centenary Chapel (*Rev. Thomas Dixon*)	281	399
United Methodist Free Church—		
Cannon Street-road (*Rev. W. J. Christophers*)	114	87
Primitive Methodist—		
Sutton-street (*Rev. Thomas Humphries*)	*59	103
Lutheran—		
Swedish Church, Princes-square (*Rev. A. R. Frost*)	61	—
Roman Catholic—		
SS. Mary and Michael, Commercial-road (*Rev. F. O. Callaghan.*)	325	475

MILE-END OLD TOWN.

	M.	E.
Church of England—		
Christ Church, Stepney (*Rev. F. J. Hobbins*)	385	243
St. Augustine, Settle-street (*Rev. H. W. Wilson*)	162	221
St. Philip, Turner-street, Stepney (*Rev. S. Vatcher*)	*315	720
St. Thomas, Harbour-square (*Rev. A. W. Cribb*)	92	106
St. Anthony, Globe-road (*Rev. A. W. F. Martell*)	162	183
St. Benet, Mile End-road (*Rev. T. Richardson*)	249	148
St. Luke, Burdett-road (*Rev. W. Wallace*)	99	250
St. Paul, Bow-common (*Rev. R. T. Plummer*)	640	580
St. Peter, Mile-end (*Rev. F. H. Dinnis*)	180	123
Holy Trinity, Tredegar-square (*Rev. J. Greaves*)	*245	188
Congregational—		
Mile End-road (*Rev. G. Seymour*)	168	248
Latimer Chapel, Bridge-street (*Rev. J. W. Atkinson*)	324	346
Burdett-road (*Rev. J. R. Fisher*)	272	434
Stepney Meeting House (*Rev. G. S. Reaney*)	511	933
Wycliffe Chapel, Stepney (*Rev. C. Lemoine*)	*642	917
Calvinistic Congregational—		
Zion Chapel, White Horse-lane, Stepney (*Various*)	29	38
Baptist—		
East London Tabernacle (*Rev. A. G. Brown*)	*1696	1831
Rehoboth Chapel, Stepney (*Various*)	117	134
Wesleyan—		
Lycett Memorial Chapel (*Rev. Cæsar Caine*)	374	412
German Wesleyan, Commercial-road (*Rev. J. Urech*)	84	97
United Methodist Free Church—		
Free Church, Jubilee-street (*Rev. W. J. Christophers*)	77	72

	M.	E.
Primitive Methodist—		
Tabernacle, Stepney-green (*Rev. Thomas Humphries*)	168	185
Church of Scotland—		
St Andrew, Philpot-street (*Rev. Dr. Souter*)	17	26
Presbyterian—		
John Knox's Church, Stepney (*Rev. James Mackintosh*)	124	131
Unitarian—		
College Chapel, Stepney-green (*Rev. R. Spears*)	73	103
Christadelphian—		
Christadelphian Hall (*Various*)	30	34
Roman Catholic—		
St. Boniface (German), Union-street (*Rev. H. Volk*)	344	407
Guardian Angels, Mile End-road (*Rev. Thomas Denny*)	197	199

STEPNEY.

COMPRISING THE SUB-DISTRICTS OF SHADWELL, RATCLIFFE, AND LIMEHOUSE.

	M.	E.
Church of England—		
St. Paul, High-street, Shadwell (*Rev. E. Bray*)	259	137
St. Dunstan, High-street (*Rev. E. Hoskyns*)	*847	1466
St. James, Ratcliff (*Rev. R. K. Arbuthnot*)	146	140
St. Matthew, Commercial-rd. East (*Rev. S. B. Bridges*)	105	179
Emmanuel Mission Church, Devonport-st., Commercial-road (*Rev. John T. Wyatt*)	113	102
St. John, Wapping (*Rev. A. R. Carter*)	186	218
St. Ann, Commercial-road (*Rev. W. Donne*)	696	851
St. John, Limehouse (*Rev. C. Anderson*)	65	84
Congregational—		
Coverdale Chapel, Commercial-street (*Rev. J. Lucas*)	172	344
Wesleyan—		
Brunswick Chapel, Limehouse (*Rev. William Hirst*)	163	210
Seamen's Chapel, Commercial-road East (*Rev. Henry W. Jones.*)	76	125
United Methodist Free Church—		
Piggot-street, Limehouse (*Rev. W. J. Christophers*)	208	137
New Jerusalem Church—		
Zion Chapel, Three Colt-street (*Various*)	—	46
Friends—		
Ratcliff Meeting House (*Various*)	54	87
Roman Catholic—		
St. Patrick, Wapping (*Rev. Francis C. Beckley*)	424	15

POPLAR.

COMPRISING THE SUB-DISTRICTS OF BOW, BROMLEY, AND POPLAR.

	M.	E.
Church of England—		
All Saints, East India-road (Rev. T. W. Nowell)	502	591
Christ Church, Isle of Dogs (Rev. C. S. Coldwell)	182	185
St. John, Isle of Dogs (Rev. E. N. Stott)	314	532
St. Luke, Millwall (Rev. J. Hewlett)	302	223
St. Matthias, High-street (Rev. C. Neil)	202	266
St. Saviour, Northumberland-street (Rev. V. E. Skrine)	210	257
St. Stephen, East India-road (Rev. R. J. Elliott)	316	314
St. Mary, Garford-street (Rev. P. Alpe)	225	215
St. Mark, Victoria-park (Rev. M. Sweetman)	169	231
St. Mary, Bow (Rev. W. P. Insley)	178	202
St. Paul, Old Ford (Rev. W. Adamson)	55	89
St. Stephen, Tredegar-road (Rev. T. R. Lawrence)	671	1138
All Hallows, Bromley-by-Bow (Rev. J. Matthews)	159	183
St. Gabriel, Bromley (Rev. F. Kirton)	290	347
St. Mary, High-street, Bromley	325	433
St. Michael, Bromley (Rev. H. M. Tyrwhitt)	436	489
All Hallows, East India Docks (Rev. A. E. Dalton)	555	704
Congregational—		
Trinity Chapel, East India-road (Rev. J. Chadburn)	520	569
Millwall Chapel, West Ferry-road (Rev. W. J. Temple)	109	167
North Bow Congregational Church (Rev. E. Schnadhorst)	68	129
Harley-street (Rev. W. E. Hurndall)	695	954
Bromley Chapel, Bruce-road (Rev. W. Saunders)	270	326
Baptist—		
Bow Chapel, High-street (Rev. G. H. Carr)	242	303
Cotton-street Chapel (Rev. W. H. Broad)	255	434
Bethel Chapel, High-street (Rev. H. F. Noyes)	60	81
Evan-street Chapel	105	367
Parnell-road, Old Ford (Rev. C. F. Vernon)	65	60
George-street, Bromley	249	643
Mount Zion, Botolph-road, Bromley (Rev. W. H. Lee)	74	107
The Tabernacle, Bromley (Rev. W. T. Lambourne)	173	299
Blackthorn-street, Bow Common (Rev. H. A. Fletcher)	251	265
Wesleyan—		
Bow-road (Rev. Edward S. Banham)	367	362
Bow Common (Rev. T. F. Rawlings)	249	234
Old Ford-road (Rev. William Hirst)	311	407
Poplar Chapel, East India-road	462	700
Cubitt Town (Rev. Thomas Dixon)	224	450
Chenal-street, Millwall (Rev. William Hirst)	95	61

THE RELIGIOUS CENSUS OF LONDON.

United Methodist Free Church—   *M.*   *E.*
   Bruce-road (*Rev. Matthias T. Myers*) . . . . 232 . 245
   Bath-street (*Rev. A. Soothill*) . . . . 414 . 590

Primitive Methodist—
   Driffield-road (*Rev. John Dickenson*) . . . 273 . 269
   Chrisp-street, Poplar (*Rev. J. R. Travener*) . . 260 . 213
   Maria-street, Millwall (*Rev. J. Tryon Davies*) . 55 . 76
   Manchester-road, Cubitt Town (*Rev. John Dickenson*). 134 . 205

Bible Christian—
   Blair-street, Poplar (*Rev. W. Jeffery*) . . . 109 . 168

Presbyterian—
   St. Paul, West Ferry-road, Millwall (*Rev. T. J. Dixon*) 54 . 43
   East India-road, Poplar (*Rev. W. H. Edmonds*) . . 133 . 109
   Mornington-road, Bow-road (*Rev. W. Michael Smith*). 89 . 116

Lutheran—
   King-street, Poplar, Danish Church . . . . Closed.
      (*Rev. William Steinthal*.)

Roman Catholic—
   Our Lady and St. Catherine, High-street . . 207 . 309
      (*Rev Dr. Thos. P. Thacker.*)
   SS. Mary and Joseph, Poplar (*Rev. James Lawless*) . 214 . 531
   St. Edmund, Millwall (*Rev. Nicholas P. Drewe*) . 167 . 144

Workhouse and Hospital Chapels—
   Stepney Workhouse (*Rev. J. Fawcett*). . . 200 . 200
   Poplar Workhouse (*Rev. R. J. Elliott*). . . 320 . —
   City of London Union Infirmary (*Rev. P. Prescott*) . 67 . 75

HACKNEY.

Comprising the Sub-Districts of Stoke Newington, Stamford Hill, West Hackney, Hackney, and South Hackney.

Church of England—
   St. Faith, Stoke Newington (*Rev. C. H. V. Pixell*) . 302 . 445
   St. John, Stamford-hill (*Rev. R. Letts*) . . 421 . 456
   St. Ann, Stamford-hill (*Rev. J. D. Letts*) . . 346 . 304
   St. Matthew, Upper Clapton (*Rev. C. H. Bradford*) . 866 . 806
   St. Mary, Stoke Newington (Old Church) . . 383 . 413
      (*Rev. T. Jackson.*)
   St. Mary, Stoke Newington (Parish Church). . 1092 . 1263
      (*Rev. L. E. Shelford.*)
   St. Michael and Angels, Stoke Newington . . 880 . 920
      (*Rev. T. Edwin Howlett.*)
   Parish Church, West Hackney (*Rev. C. J. Robinson*) . 1040 . 960
   St. Matthias, Stoke Newington (*Rev. F. Cauldwell*) . 223 . 249
   St. Philip, Richmond-road, Dalston (*Rev. F. Cox*) . 380 . 395

HACKNEY.

	M.	E.
Church of England (continued)—		
All Saints, Stoke Newington (*Rev. H. Shrimpton*)	492	516
St. Andrew, South Hackney (*Rev. G. Robinson*)	290	228
Eton Mission Church, South Hackney	181	331
(*Rev. Wm. Marlb. Carter.*)		
St. Augustine, Victoria-park (*Rev. E. W. J. Bankes*)	333	436
St. John of Jerusalem, South Hackney	592	758
(*Rev. J. H. Lester.*)		
St. Barnabas, Homerton (*Rev. F. R. Blatch*)	287	301
All Souls, Clapton Park (*Rev. F. H. A. Hawkins*)	373	350
Episcopal Chapel, Homerton (*Rev. W. Baker*)	295	249
St. Luke, Hackney (*Rev. W. H. Langhorne*)	813	800
St. Michael, South Hackney (*Rev. J. B. Podmore*)	360	283
Christ Church, Victoria Park (*Rev. J. C. Egan*)	333	209
All Saints, Clapton Park (*Rev. B. M. Kitson*)	663	634
Christ Church, Clapton (*Rev. G. P. Read*)	388	120
St. James, Lower Clapton (*Rev. H. D. Pearson*)	554	282
St. Bartholomew, Dalston-lane (*Rev. J. G. Pilkington*)	407	472
Holy Trinity, Dalston (*Rev. R. S. Hassard*)	461	465
St. John-at-Hackney (*Rev. A. Brook*)	1093	963
St. Thomas, Clapton-common (*Rev. F. W. Kingsford*)	425	239
Almshouse Chapel, Kingsland-road	33	a20
St. Mark, Dalston (*Rev. J. G. Pilkington*)	796	726
St. Peter, Kingsland (*Rev. C. J. Finch*)	328	507
St. Andrew, Stamford-hill (*Rev. H. E. J. Bevan*)	745	549
Refuge for the Destitute, Dalston	48	48
Congregational—		
Kingsland Congregational Church (*Vacant*)	430	456
Bethesda, Stamford-hill (*Various*)	98	90
Raleigh Memorial, Stoke Newington (*Rev. J. Johnston*)	282	290
Clapton Church, Upper Clapton (*Rev. H. J. Gamble*)	359	254
Gohebydd Memorial, Stoke Newington (*Various*)	—	53
Clapton Park Chapel, Hackney (*Rev. W. J. Woods*)	845	659
St. Thomas'-square (*Rev. Henry Varley*)	109	141
Chatsworth Road Tabernacle (*Vacant*)	350	447
Cambridge Heath (*Rev. W. Marshall*)	296	244
Victoria Park Tabernacle (*Rev. George Snashall*)	404	442
St. Thomas Hall (*Rev. Samuel Hester*)	215	270
Bethany, South Hackney	129	129
Old Gravel Pit (*Rev. J. de K. Williams*)	309	279
Amherst-road (*Vacant*)	310	248
Shrubland-road, Dalston (*Rev. T. C. Udall*)	133	226
Middleton-road, Dalston (*Rev. W. J. Evans*)	343	403
Southgate-road Chapel (*Rev. R. H. Noble*)	204	237
Abney Congregational (*Rev. W. Spensely*)	595	642
Rectory-road (*Rev. C. F. Williams*)	374	384
Stamford-hill Church (*Rev. R. V. Pryce*)	615	446
Trinity Chapel, Hackney (*Vacant*)	510	248

		M.	E.
Baptist—			
Devonshire-square (*Rev. E. H. Ellis*)		1008	1194
Ashwin-street, Dalston (*Rev. W. H. Burton*)		693	770
Downs-road, Hackney (*Rev. T. V. Tymms*)		480	432
Chatsworth-road (*Various*)		103	61
Forest-road, Hackney (*Various*)		87	92
Homerton-row, Hackney (*Rev. J. Bennett*)		69	51
Hampden Chapel (*Rev. J. Hillman*)		156	147
Mallard-street Chapel (*Vacant*)		—	17
Mare-street (*Rev. Evan Thomas*)		462	568
Wellington-road (*Various*)		57	61
Woodberry Down (*Rev. W. R. Skerry*)		440	503
Bouverie-road (*Rev. G. H. Malins*)		52	57
Wesleyan—			
Lower Clapton (*Rev. George Kenyon*)		524	475
Richmond-road Chapel (*Rev. W. D. Wallers*)		376	427
Cassland-road Chapel (*Rev. Marshall Hartley*)		579	518
Hackney Wick (*Rev. Marshall Hartley*)		190	250
Green Lanes (*Rev. W. T. Slater*)		541	321
Mayfield-terrace, Dalston (*Rev. Robt. P. Downes*)		374	404
United Methodist Free Church—			
Methodist Free Church, Stoke Newington		37	62
(*Rev. Thomas Foster.*)			
Pembury-grove (*Rev. William Trevail*)		163	134
Primitive Methodist—			
Brookfield-road (*Rev. G. Shapcott*)		112	124
Stoke Newington-common (*Rev. Thomas Guttery*)		85	73
London Fields (*Rev. G. Shapcott*)		106	74
Blurton-road (*Rev. George B. Gleghorn*)		204	243
Castle-street, Kingsland (*Rev. G. Shapcott*)		118	162
Presbyterian—			
Downs Park-road, Clapton (*Rev. M. Davison*)		170	98
Lordship-road, Stoke Newington (*Rev. A. C. Alexander*)		253	175
Friends—			
Park-street (*Various*)		171	76
Catholic Apostolic—			
Mare-street, Hackney (*Rev. Herbert Heath*)		227	168
Christian Church—			
Loddiges-road (*Various*)		37	43
Unitarian—			
Newington-green (*Rev. W. Wooding*)		93	71
New Gravel-pit		148	77
New Jerusalem Church—			
Albion Hall, Dalston (*Rev. C. Fairweather*)		37	25

	M.	E.

German Lutheran—
Ritson-road, Dalston (*Rev. Dr. Adolphus Walbaum*) . — . 120

Undenominational—
Speldhurst-road (*Vacant*) . . . . . . 212 . 351

Roman Catholic—
St. John the Baptist (*Rev. William Fleming*) . . 191 . 175
Church of the Immaculate Heart, Homerton . . 211 . 308
  (*Rev. Thomas W. Hogan.*)
St. Scholastica, Clapton (*Rev. Robert Swift*) . . 128 . 140
Church of Our Lady and St. Joseph (*Rev. Jas. Hussey*) 428 . 220

Workhouse—
City of London Workhouse (*Rev. H. S. Roberts*) . . 142 . 124

ST. PANCRAS.

COMPRISING THE SUB-DISTRICTS OF REGENT'S PARK, TOTTENHAM COURT ROAD, GRAY'S-INN LANE, SOMERS TOWN, CAMDEN TOWN, AND KENTISH TOWN.

Church of England—
Kentish Town Parish Church (*Rev. J. C. Cowd*) . . 563 . 666
St. Barnabas, Kentish Town (*Rev. H. E. Whish*) . . 465 . 627
Camden Town Parish Church (*Rev. J. Fitzgerald*) . 90 . 74
St. Anne, Highgate-rise (*Rev. C. T. Ackland*) . . 360 . 318
Trinity Church, Gray's-inn-road (*Rev. F. Thorne*) . 127 . 195
The Holy Cross, Dutton-street (*Rev. A. Moore*) . . 110 . —
St. Peter, Regent-square (*Rev. R. H. A. Bradley*) . 169 . 173
Holy Trinity, Haverstock-hill (*Rev. E. L. Cutts*) . 491 . 552
St. Andrew, Haverstock-hill (*Rev. C. G. Blaxland*) . 300 . 362
St. Augustine, Highgate (*Rev. E. Smith*) . . . 174 . 242
St. Benet, Kentish Town (*Rev. F. O. Rowland*) . . 249 . 236
St. John, Haverstock-hill . . . . 100 . 120
St. Luke, Caversham-road (*Rev. C. H. Andrews*) . . *647 . 1115
St. Martin, Haverstock-hill (*Rev. J. G. Medland*) . . 179 . 113
St. Mary, Highgate-rise (*Rev. D. J. T. Cooke*) . . 871 . 961
St. Paul, Camden-square (*Rev. E. R. Adams*) . . 702 . 754
St. Thomas, Kentish Town (*Rev. R. P. Clemenger*) . 312 . 199
St. Silas, Kentish Town . . . . 67 . 87
St. Michael, Camden-road (*Rev. E. B. Penfold*) . . 230 . 312
St. Pancras, Old Church (*Rev. W. R. Arrowsmith*) . 85 . 88
Christ Church, Albany-street (*Rev. J. W. Festing*) . 1098 . 873
St. Mark, Gloucester-gate (*Rev. W. B. Galloway*) . 274 . 204
St. Bede, Little Albany-street (*Various*) . . . 73 . 402
St. Bartholomew, Gray's-inn-road (*Rev. R. J. Bird*) . 174 . 189
St. Jude, Gray's-inn-road (*Rev. J. M. Andrews*) . . 513 . 771
All Saints, Gordon-square (*Rev. A. R. Godson*) . . 155 . 170
St. John, Fitzroy-square (*Rev. J. J. Coxhead*) . . 127 . 219
St. Pancras, Euston-road (*Rev. H. D. M. Spence*) . . 1759 . 2198

Church of England (*continued*)—   M.   E.
St. Mary Magdalene, Munster-square . . . 328 . 269
    (*Rev. F. J. Ponsonby.*)
St. Saviour, Fitzroy-square (*Rev. T. Turner*) . . 285 . 430
Christ Church, Charlton-street (*Rev. F. S. O'Brien*) . 165 . 226
St. James, Hampstead-road (*Rev. C. W. Hodson*) . 110 . 127
St. Mary, Seymour-street (*Rev. T. Stevenson*) . . 165 . 200
St. Matthew, Oakley-square (*Rev. C. Philips*) . . 299 . 279

Congregational—
Highgate Congregational Church (*Rev. J. M. Gibbon*) . 672 . 540
St. Paul's, Hawley-road, Kentish Town (*Rev. E. White*) 409 . 371
Haverstock Church, Haverstock-hill (*Rev. J. Nunn*) . 606 . 296
Kentish Town-road (*Rev. T. M. Mundle*) . . . 627 . 867
Gospel Oak Chapel (*Rev. H. Le Pla*) . . . . 237 . 350
Park Chapel, Camden Town (*Rev. J. C. Harrison*) . 757 . 724
Tottenham Court-road Chapel (*Rev. J. Jackson Wray*). 733 . 1242
Bedford New Town Church (*Rev. J. L. Phillips*) . . 387 . 390
Tolmers-square, Hampstead-road (*Rev. F. Hastings*) . 587 . 684

Baptist—
Arthur-street, King's-cross-road (*Rev. W. Smith*) . . 130 . 220
Highgate-road (*Rev. J. Stephens*) . . . . . 589 . 677
Malden-road . . . . 180 . 131
Camden-street (*Rev. George Haidler*) . . . . 69 . 50
Great College-street (*Rev. R. Burbidge*) . . . 194 . 131
Chalk Farm Chapel (*Rev. G. Scudamore*) . . . 303 . 308
Henrietta-street, Brunswick-square (*Rev. W. J. Taylor*) 71 . 79
Gower-street Chapel (*Various*) . . . . . 330 . 382

Wesleyan—
Liverpool-street, King's-cross (*Rev. James F. Pyle*) . 376 . 480
Prince of Wales's-road (*Rev. John H. Sholl*) . . 652 . 750
Lady Margaret-road (*Rev. W. J. Tweddle*) . . . 317 . 219
Camden-street (*Rev. Joseph Garrett*) . . . . 150 . 230

Primitive Methodist—
Primitive Methodist Church, King-street . . . 134 . 242
    (*Rev. Thomas Guttery.*)
Winchester-street, King's-cross (*Various*) . . . 92 . 201

Presbyterian—
Trinity Church, Kentish Town-road . . . . 264 . 467
    (*Rev. C. J. Whitmore.*)
Oxendon Church, Haverstock-hill (*Rev. D. C. Sillars*) . 289 . 253
Camden-road (*Rev. R. M. Thornton*) . . . . 417 . 323
Regent-square (*Rev. Dr. Dykes*) . . . . . 913 . 1532
Ossulton-street, Somers Town (*Rev. Z. B. Woffendale*) 629 . 715

German Lutheran—
St. Mary, Fitzroy-square (*Rev. C. Schoell*) . . . 247   169

	M.	*E.*
New Jerusalem Church—		
Argyle-square (*Rev. J. Presland*) . . .	131	134
Catholic Apostolic—		
Gospel Oak	203	54
Gordon-square, Tottenham Court-road . . .	168	137
(*Rev. Henry Hume.*)		
Disciples of Christ—		
Hope Chapel, Prince of Wales'-road . . .	111	109
Unitarian—		
Clarence-road, Kentish Town (*Rev. J. P. Ham*) . .	91	118
Roman Catholic—		
St. Aloysius Chapel, Clarendon-square . .	435	338
(*Rev. Edmund Pennington*)		
St. Anne's Church, Little Albany-street. .	114	62
(*Rev. Frederick Bown*)		
Our Lady, Kentish Town (*Rev. James Connolly*) . .	209	310
St. Dominic's, Haverstock-hill (*Rev. E. A. Williams*) .	423	763
Hospitals, Workhouses, etc.—		
St. Pancras Workhouse Chapel (*Rev. F. Leedham*) .	200	200
Foundling Hospital Chapel (*Rev. A. W. Momerie*) .	849	—
St. Pancras Infirmary Chapel	62	40

HAMPSTEAD.

Church of England—		
Trinity Church (*Rev. H. Sharpe*)	1100	950
St. Stephen, Hampstead-green (*Rev. J. Kirkman*) .	752	620
St. Peter, Belsize-park, Hampstead . . .	934	534
(*Rev. F. W. Tremlett.*)		
St. John, Church-row (*Rev. S. B. Burnaby*) . .	754	753
St. John's Chapel, Downshire-hill (*Rev. G. S. Karney*)	288	262
Emmanuel Church (*Rev. E. Davys*) . . .	249	171
St. Cuthbert (*Rev. E. Davys*)	253	138
St. James	215	208
Christ Church (*Rev. G. F. Head*)	1137	1188
St. Mary, King Henry's-road (*Rev. C. J. Fuller*) .	148	133
All Souls, St. John's Wood, *Rev. H. R. Wadmore*)	274	176
St. Saviour, Haverstock-hill (*Rev. G. H. Herklots*)	398	423
St. Mary, Kilburn (*Rev. J. Robertson*) . .	859	585
St. Paul, Regent's-park (*Rev. J. W. Bennett*) .	719	367
Congregational—		
Congregational Church, Lyndhurst-road . .	857	1165
(*Rev. R. F. Horton.*)		
New College Chapel, St. John's Wood (*Rev. J. Barker*)	221	128

	M.	E.
Baptist—		
Brondesbury Chapel (*Rev. J. C. Thompson*).	421	453
Ebenezer Chapel, New-end (*Vacant*)	53	47
Heath-street Chapel (*Rev. W. Brock*).	457	351
Wesleyan—		
High-street (*Rev. R. J. Andrew*).	332	297
Quex-road, Kilburn (*Rev. David Roe*).	356	400
Presbyterian—		
Trinity Church, High-street (*Vacant*).	348	146
Unitarian—		
Roslyn Hill Chapel (*Rev. Dr. Sadler*).	216	155
United Christians—		
Ebenezer Chapel, Kilburn Vale (*Various*).	65	54
Roman Catholic—		
St. Mary's Church (*Rev. A. D. G. Purcell*).	206	65
Church of the Sacred Heart.	220	203
Workhouse—		
Hampstead Workhouse Chapel (*Rev. G. H. Herklots*).	—	80

KENSINGTON.

Comprising Sub-districts of St. Mary, Paddington; St. John, Paddington; Kensington Town; Brompton.

	M.	E.
Church of England—		
St. Michael, Paddington (*Rev. G. S. Prescott*)	975	663
St. John, Oxford-square (*Rev. Sir G. R. Bayley*).	727	593
St. James, Sussex-gardens (*Rev. W. Abbott*)	697	518
Christ Church, Lancaster-gate (*Rev. C. J. Ridgeway*).	1593	1295
All Saints, Norfolk-square (*Rev. J. Maconechy*).	156	148
St. Matthew, Bayswater (*Rev. J. F. Sullivan*)	1342	1182
Holy Trinity, Bishops-road (*Rev. D. Moore*)	1265	1081
St. Mary, Paddington-green (*Rev. A. Scott*).	270	356
St. Philip, Edgware-road (*Rev. A. Scott*)	165	89
St. Stephen, Westbourne Park-road (*Rev. T. B. H. Brooks.*)	1490	1115
St. Mary Magdalene, Woodchester-street (*Rev. R. T. West.*)	1005	1100
St. Thomas, Westbourne-grove (*Rev. Percy H. Collins*)	288	199
St. Saviour, Warwick-road (*Rev. M. Tweddell*).	1350	700
St. Luke, Canterbury-road (*Rev. R. Williams*).	256	280
St. Peter, Chippenham-road (*Rev. W. H. Hodge*)	604	578
St. Augustine, Kilburn Park-road (*Rev. C. Kirkpatrick*)	866	785
St. Paul, Harrow-road (*Rev. H. Cowell*)	590	680
St. Luke, Westbourne Park (*Rev. J. Knowles*)	354	395
Emmanuel Church, Harrow-road (*Rev. R. Faraker*).	280	362

KENSINGTON. 33

	M.	E.
Church of England *(continued)*—		
St. Mary Abbott, High-street (*Hon. & Rev. E. C. Glyn*)	1970	1830
St. Gabriel (*Rev. A. Williamson*)	283	425
Christ Church, Victoria-road (*Hon. & Rev. E. C. Glyn*)	567	166
St. Paul, Vicarage-gardens (*Hon. & Rev. E. C. Glyn*)	355	150
St. George, Notting Hill-green (*Rev. C. A. Leveson*)	685	452
St. Peter, Kensington Park-road (*Rev. C. M. Moore*)	915	518
St. John, Ladbroke-grove (*Rev. Dr. Thornton*)	797	445
St. James, Addison-road North (*Rev. A. Williamson*)	907	739
St. John, Holland-road (*Rev. George Booker*)	738	248
St. Helen, North Kensington (*Rev. A. D. Robinson*)	413	274
SS. Andrew and Philip (*Rev. R. Towers*)	233	342
All Saints, Kensington Park (*Rev. W. F. Trench*)	760	784
St. Clement, Notting Hill (*Rev. E. Hoskyns*)	239	515
St. Michael, Ladbroke Grove-road (*Rev. Dr. Gray*)	474	400
Christ Church, Notting Hill (*Rev. E. Clarke*)	195	304
St. Mark, Notting Hill (*Rev. E. W. Emmet*)	512	474
St. Jude, South Kensington (*Rev. R. W. Forrest*)	1450	1020
St. Matthias, Earl's Court (*Rev. W. H. C. Luke*)	854	1159
Holy Trinity, Brompton-road (*Rev. W. Covington*)	624	486
St. Peter, Cranley-gardens, Brompton	1250	433
(*Hon. and Rev. F. E. C. Byng*)		
Brompton Chapel, Montpelier-street	102	126
(*Rev. W. Covington*)		
St. Paul, Onslow-square (*Rev. H. W. Webb-Peploe*)	1802	1174
St. Mary Boltons, West Brompton	697	760
(*Rev. W. T. Du Boulay.*)		
St. Augustine, South Kensington (*Rev. R. R. Chope*)	610	265
St. Stephen, South Kensington (*Rev. J. P. Waldo*)	957	450
St. Philip, Earl's Court-road (*Rev. W. Smale*)	785	967
St. Cuthbert, Philbeach-gardens (*Rev. H. Westall*)	385	369
St. Luke, Redcliffe-square (*Rev. Wm. Fraser Handcock*)	484	264
St. Barnabas (*Rev. George R. Thornton*)	956	509
Congregational—		
Craven-terrace, Bayswater (*Rev. D. M. Jenkins*)	286	361
Horbury Church, Notting Hill (*Rev. W. Roberts*)	371	430
Allen-street, Kensington (*Rev. Colmer B. Symes*)	584	479
Golborne-road, North Kensington (*Rev. H. R. Davis*)	284	545
Walmer-road, Notting Hill (*Various*)	88	101
Union—		
Norland Chapel, Notting Hill (*Rev. H. J. Weatherhead*)	220	701
Baptist—		
Tabernacle, Praed-street, Paddington (*Rev. G. Robinson*)	191	317
Shirland-road, St. Peter's Park (*Rev. J. M. Cox*)	100	96
Bosworth-road	132	165
Beulah Chapel, Harrow-road (*Rev. J. Munns*)	65	97
Ladbroke-grove (*Rev. R. H. Roberts*)	460	520

Baptist (continued)—

	M.	E.
Kensington-place, Notting Hill (*Rev. G. Herring*)	27	38
Westbourne Grove Church (*Rev. J. Tuckwell*)	417	545
Thistle-grove, Fulham-road (*Rev. A. Brandon*)	85	114
Onslow Chapel, Queen's Elm (*Rev. S. A. Swaine*)	170	155
Westbourne Park (*Rev. Dr. Clifford*)	1023	1456

Wesleyan—

	M.	E.
Sutherland-gardens (*Rev. Sampson Weaver*)	641	762
Lancaster-road, Notting Hill (*Rev. Wm. R. Bevan*)	296	670
Clarence-place, Kensington (*Rev. John Reacher*)	169	101
Warwick-gardens (*Rev. John Bartley*)	220	310
Denbigh-road (*Rev. Joseph Olphert*)	489	511

United Methodist Free Church—

	M.	E.
Queen's-road, Bayswater (*Rev. William Howe*)	113	125
Cambridge-road, Kilburn (*Rev. J. Wright*)	114	205

Primitive Methodist—

	M.	E.
Fowel-street, Notting Hill (*Rev. Thomas B. Corkwell*)	86	103

Presbyterian—

	M.	E.
Trinity Church, Notting Hill (*Rev. H. S. Paterson*)	417	331
Scarsdale Villas, Kensington (*Rev. C. Moinet*)	243	193
St. Paul, Bayswater (*Rev. Dr. Morison*)	189	360
Cornwall-gardens (*Rev. V. M. White*)	205	160

Undenominational—

	M.	E.
West London Tabernacle, Notting Hill (*Rev. W. T. Moore.*)	385	595
Talbot Tabernacle, Notting Hill (*Vacant*)	383	489

New Jerusalem Church—

	M.	E.
Palace-gardens-terrace, Kensington (*Various*)	296	333

Welsh Calvinistic Methodist—

	M.	E.
Shirland-road, St. Peter's-park (*Various*)	125	200

Unitarian—

	M.	E.
The Mall, Notting Hill (*Rev. W. Carey Walters*)	39	36

French Evangelical Protestant—

	M.	E.
Monmouth-road (*Rev. H. P. de la Harpe*)	73	52

Catholic Apostolic—

	M.	E.
Harrow-road, Paddington Green	260	200

Greek Church—

	M.	E.
Moscow-road (*Rev. Dr. D. Plaisas*)	179	—

Roman Catholic—

	M.	E.
Our Lady (*Rev. A. L. M. Echevarria*)	171	255
Mary of the Angels (*Rev. Francis J. Kirk*)	548	475
St. Francis (*Rev. Cuthbert Robinson*)	258	454

		M.	*E.*
Roman Catholic *(continued)*			
Pro-Cathedral, High-street (*Rev. Michael Fanning*)		475	631
Carmelite Church (*Rev. Wm. Thomas Gordon*)		223	555
Oratory, Brompton (*Rev. Wm. Thomas Gordon*)		1840	2030
Sacred and Sorrowful Heart, etc.		265	348
Jews—			
West-end Synagogue (*Rev. Simeon Singer*)		161	—
Bayswater Synagogue (*Rev. Isaac Samuel*)		261	—
Workhouse and Hospitals—			
Paddington Workhouse Chapel		65	64
Lock Hospital Chapel, Harrow-road		480	378
(*Rev. Dr. F. Smith-Cook.*)			
Kensington Workhouse Chapel		208	192
Kensington Workhouse Chapel (Roman Catholic)		172	—
Marylebone Infirmary ,, ,,		125	—
St. Luke (Consumption Hospital) ,, ,,		240	160

FULHAM.

Comprising the Sub-Districts of St. Peter, Hammersmith; St. Paul, Hammersmith; Fulham.

	M.	*E.*
Church of England—		
Christ Church, Blythe-road, West Kensington-park	520	440
(*Rev. W. Handcock.*)		
St. Peter, Fulham (*Rev. R. Cardwell*)	421	384
St. Mary, Hammersmith (*Rev. J. Macnaught*)	624	318
St. John, Walham-green (*Rev. E. Batty*)	442	500
St. James, Fulham (*Rev. W. H. Denny*)	112	148
St. Andrew, Fulham (*Rev. J. H. Cardwell*)	785	697
All Saints, Fulham (*Rev. F. H. Fisher*)	700	850
St. Mary, Stamford Brook-road	392	269
(*Rev. W. E. F. Greene.*)		
St. Luke, Shepherd's-bush (*Rev. H. Rowswell*)	719	562
Holy Innocents, Dalling-road (*Rev. J. Staffurth*)	261	357
St. Stephens, Uxbridge-road (*Rev. W. L. Collett*)	550	535
St. John, Clenthorne-road (*Rev. W. A. Whitworth*)	560	591
St. Peter, Hammersmith (*Rev. G. H. Tidcombe*)	193	106
St. Thomas, Shepherd's-bush (*Rev. H. Small*)	502	370
St. Mark, St. James-street (*Rev. J. H. Snowden*)	145	279
St. Matthew, Addison-gardens (*Rev. W. Handcock*)	426	293
St. Paul, Queen-street, Broadway (*Rev. J. H. Snowden*)	647	596
St. Simon, West Kensington-park (*Rev. R. Handcock*)	505	348
Congregational—		
West Kensington (*Rev. A. Norris*)	298	249
Oaklands, Shepherd's-bush (*Rev. W. Sanders*)	234	215
Broadway Chapel (*Rev. R. Macbeth*)	120	102

Baptist—

	M.	E.
West-end, Hammersmith (*Rev. W. Page*)	279	229
Addison-park (*Rev. P. W. Williamson*)	93	68

Wesleyan—

Salem Chapel, Walham-green (*Rev. W. Brunyate*)	170	378
Munster-park (*Rev. John C. Stanfield*)	294	226
West Kensington-park (*Rev. John Reacher*)	338	346
River-court, King-street West (*Rev. John Bartley*)	466	435
Bassein-park Church (*Rev. Robert Foster*)	234	304

United Methodist Free Church—

Walham-grove (*Rev. William Howe*)	115	66
Ebenezer Church, Fulham (*Rev. G. W. Bishop*)	119	190

Methodist New Connexion—

Bethel Chapel, Fulham (*Rev. Dr. C. D. Ward*)	234	150

Primitive Methodist—

Dalling-road (*Rev. Joseph Sheale*)	115	60

Presbyterian—

St. Andrew, Leysfield-road (*Rev. H. Miller*)	305	218

Free Church—

Starch Green-road	189	196

Friends—

Middle Mall, Hammersmith (*Various*)	54	19

Christadelphian—

Broxholm-road, Fulham (*Various*)	—	47

Roman Catholic—

St. Thomas of Canterbury (*Rev. Alexius Mills*)	228	297
Most Holy Trinity (*Rev. Alfred White*)	351	208

WANDSWORTH.

COMPRISING THE SUB-DISTRICTS OF CLAPHAM, BATTERSEA, WANDSWORTH, PUTNEY, AND STREATHAM.

Church of England—

	M.	E.
Iron Temporary Church, Streatham	267	148
Church of the Ascension, Balham-hill (*Rev. H. Curtis*)	733	585
St. Stephen, Streatham (*Rev. G. Eastman*)	399	283
St. Peter, Streatham (*Rev. A. C. Tarbutt*)	588	566
St. Nicholas, Tooting	450	332
St. Mary, Balham-hill (*Rev. T. Bates*)	754	576
St. Leonard, Streatham (*Rev. J. R. Nicholl*)	1130	985
Emmanuel, Streatham-common (*Rev. G. S. Streathfield*)	1100	786
Holy Trinity, Upper Tooting (*Rev. J. H. Potter*)	745	466
Christ Church, Roupell-park (*Rev. W. B. A. Raven*)	507	311
St. John, Putney-hill (*Hon. and Rev. R. Henley*)	416	223

WANDSWORTH.

	M.	E.
Church of England (*continued*)—		
All Saints, Putney (*Hon. and Rev. R. Henley*)	474	502
Holy Trinity, Roehampton (*Rev. R. Carrington*)	275	172
St. Mary, Putney (*Hon. and Rev. R. Henley*)	620	524
St. Philip, Battersea (*Rev. J. C. Lentott*)	352	576
Church of the Ascension, Lavender-hill. (*Rev. C. S. Wallace.*)	447	599
St. Saviour, Battersea (*Rev. J. G. Rice*)	277	393
St. George, Battersea (*Rev T. Lander*)	251	206
All Saints, Battersea-park (*Rev. A. E. Bourne*)	189	240
St. Andrew, Dashwood-road (*Rev. J. Holroyde*)	176	265
St. Anselm, Coventry-road (*Rev. F. A. S. Read*)	322	230
St. Alban, Streatham (*Rev. S. M. Ransom*)	298	120
St. Matthew, Lavender-hill (*Rev. C. T. Burges*)	308	373
St. Luke, Nightingale-lane (*Rev. J. Erskine Clarke*)	426	359
St. Mark, Battersea-rise (*Rev. A. C. Woodhouse*)	753	643
St. Mary, Church-road (*Rev. J. Erskine Clarke*)	430	625
St. Peter, Plough-road (*Rev. J. Miles*)	572	608
St. Mary, Bedford-hill, Balham (*Rev. P. Watson*)	416	405
Christ Church, Battersea (*Rev. H. G. Sprigg*)	363	670
St. Michael, Battersea-rise (*Rev. J. S. Barford*)	756	549
St. John, Usk-road (*Rev. J. Toone*)	254	248
St. Saviour, Cedars-road (*Rev. C. P. Greene*)	388	310
Holy Trinity, Clapham-common (*Rev. C. P. Greene*)	1061	935
St. John, Clapham-rise (*Rev. C. H. C. Baker*)	587	677
St. Paul, New Wandsworth (*Rev. E. C. Bruce*)	438	283
All Saints, Wandsworth (*Rev. H. Reed*)	452	404
Holy Trinity, West-hill (*Rev. C. P. Greene*)	480	241
St. Ann, St. Ann's-hill (*Rev. E. W. T. Chave*)	375	342
St. Andrew's, Wandsworth (*Rev. J. H. Browne*)	140	133
St. Nicholas, Lower Tooting (*Rev. E. H. Morton*)	295	163
St. Mary Magdalene, Upper Tooting (*Rev. W. S. Shuttleworth.*)	348	251
St. Stephen, Wandsworth (*Rev. C. Carruthers*)	511	303
St. Faith, Wandsworth (*Rev. R. Taylor*)	296	261
St. Michael, Merton-road	347	225
Christ Church, Union-grove (*Rev. B. Abbott*)	405	595
St. Paul, Larkhall-rise (*Rev. G. Forrester*)	806	541
St. James, Park-hill (*Rev. W. H. Barlow*)	730	610
All Saints, New Park-road (*Rev. A. G. Girdlestone*)	450	340
St. Peter, Manor-street	264	277
Congregational—		
East-hill, Wandsworth (*Rev. J. Park*)	526	483
Park-crescent, Clapham (*Rev. W. H. Edwards*)	64	48
Grafton-square, Clapham (*Rev. J. G. Rogers*)	695	544
Bridge-road, Battersea (*Rev. T. Jarratt*)	335	408
Lavender-hill (*Rev. R. Bulmer*)	321	335
Union Church, Putney (*Rev. R. A. Redford*)	255	152

Congregational (*continued*)—

	M.	E.
Oxford-road, Putney (*Rev. S. Todd*)	60	48
Balham and Upper Tooting (*Rev. J. Brierley*)	407	331
Streatham-hill (*Rev. J. Gledstone*)	284	242
Bedford-park	149	119

Union—

	M.	E.
Congregational and Baptist Church, Trinity-road	152	117
Union Tabernacle, Wandsworth-road (*Rev. D. M. Cameron.*)	193	296
Lower Tooting and Merton (*Rev. A. E. Seddon*)	138	105

Baptist—

	M.	E.
Providence Chapel, Tooting-grove (*Rev. G. Crutcher*)	50	60
Longley-road, Lower Tooting (*Rev. T. Witney*)	85	74
Lewin-road, Streatham (*Rev. J. P. Clark*)	141	165
Ramsden-road, Balham (*Rev. B. C. Etheridge*)	299	266
Trinity Chapel, Balham (*Rev. J. Brierley*)	70	63
Werter-road, Putney (*Rev. W. Thomas*)	134	202
Battersea-park Chapel (*Rev. T. Lardner*)	541	583
New Park-road (*Rev. W. H. McMechan*)	206	172
Chatham-road, Wandsworth-common (*Rev. C. E. Stone*)	193	294
Battersea Chapel, Meyrick-road (*Rev. W. Moxham*)	270	191
Battersea Chapel, York-road (*Rev. W. Hamilton*)	317	273
Surrey-lane (*Rev. G. S. Cook*)	121	153
Ebenezer Church, Wirtemberg-street (*Rev. H. Hall*)	95	74
Grafton-square (*Rev. R. Webb*)	290	185
Victoria Chapel, Wandsworth-road (*Rev. E. Henderson*)	437	594
East-hill, Wandsworth (*Rev. J. W. Ewing*)	395	390
Haldon-road, West-hill (*Rev. J. Clarke*)	77	86
Zion-hill (*Various*)	60	85

Presbyterian—

	M.	E.
Defoe Chapel, Tooting (*Rev. Dr. Anderson*)	74	73
Trinity, Clapham-road (*Rev. Dr. MacEwan*)	736	421
Granard Church, Roehampton (*Rev. D. Matheson*)	81	59
Trinity Church, Pendennis-road (*Rev. W. M. Macphail*)	196	173
Merton-road (*Rev. J. Cunningham*)	182	166

Wesleyan—

	M.	E.
St. John's-hill (*Rev. F. J. Sharr*)	725	595
Clifton-street (*Rev. William Spiers*)	29	104
Clapham Wesleyan Church (*Rev. Robert Culley*)	514	546
High-road, Upper Tooting (*Rev. A. Martyn*)	236	220
Bridge-road, Battersea (*Rev. E. Brigden*)	390	424
Queen's-road, Battersea (*Rev. Dr. F. Greeves*)	590	748
Upper Richmond-road, Putney (*Rev. John C. Stanfield*)	193	138

United Methodist Free Church—

	M.	E.
Mallinson-road, Battersea (*Rev. C. Tregourny*)	240	174
Church-road, Battersea (*Rev. J. Hocking*)	144	150
Battersea-park (*Rev. J. Roberts*)	131	120

	M.	E.
Primitive Methodist—		
High-street, Wandsworth (*Rev. Peter Coates*)	125	72
Plough-road, Battersea (*Rev. William Rowe*)	215	184
Wandsworth-road (*Rev. Peter Coates*)	98	195
Lavender-hill (*Rev. G. E. Butt*)	190	140
High-street, Putney (*Rev. William Rowe*)	89	98
Bible Christian—		
Wirtemberg-street, Clapham	63	69
Friends—		
High-street, Wandsworth (*Various*)	17	4
Unitarian—		
Unitarian Christian Church, Wandsworth (*Rev. W. G. Tarrant.*)	100	124
Free Church of England—		
Emmanuel Church, Putney (*Rev. H. O. Meyers*)	135	138
Roman Catholic—		
St. Joseph, Roehampton (*Rev. John Morris*)	147	195
Sacred Heart, West Battersea (*Rev. Wm. J. Connolly*)	337	110
Our Lady, East Battersea (*Rev. William Linnett*)	230	320
St. Thomas of Canterbury, Wandsworth (*Rev. H. D. Galleran.*)	169	170
Park-road, Clapham (*Rev. Hugh Macdonald*)	450	440
Hospitals, Workhouses, etc.—		
Magdalen Hospital Church, Streatham (*Rev. W. Watkins.*)	403	235
Lunatic Asylum, Upper Tooting	542	594
Wandsworth and Clapham Union	59	100
New Workhouse, Garratt-lane	175	139
Royal Victoria Patriotic School	270	272
H. M. Prison, Wandsworth-common	1004	1004

ISLINGTON.

COMPRISING THE SUB-DISTRICTS OF UPPER HOLLOWAY, ISLINGTON, AND HIGHBURY.

Church of England—		
Christ Church, Highbury-grove (*Rev. W. J. Chapman*)	500	334
St. Augustine, Highbury New Park (*Rev. G. Calthrop*)	1050	972
St. John, Highbury-vale (*Rev. G. Drayatt*)	481	480
St. Jude, Mildmay Park (*Rev. D. B. Hankin*)	1031	891
St. Saviour, Aberdeen Park (*Rev. John Bicknell*)	455	438
St. Thomas, Finsbury Park	275	300
St. George, Tufnell Park (*Rev. M. Washington*)	936	642
St. John, Highgate-hill (*Rev. H. W. Dearden*)	777	745

Church of England (*continued*):—	M.	E.
St. Mark, Tollington Park (*Rev. J. Hurst*)	530	555
St. Mary, Hornsey-rise (*Rev. W. S. Lewis*)	754	787
St. Paul, Kingsdown-road (*Rev. J. Piper*)	541	515
St. Peter, Anatola-road (*Rev. J. F. Osborne*)	277	390
St. Stephen, Upper Holloway (*Rev. J. Kahn*)	260	237
Whittington College Chapel (*Rev. R. A. Currey*)	19	a12
All Saints, Tufnell Park (*Rev. E. A. B. Sanders*)	452	456
St. Saviour, Upper Holloway	269	277
St. Anne, Poole's Park (*Rev. W. H. Chambers*)	486	436
St. Bartholomew, Shepperton-road (*Rev. L. Stanham*)	83	176
St. Philip, Arlington-square (*Rev. H. J. Berguer*)	200	274
St. Barnabas, Harvest-road (*Rev. F. A. C. Lillingston*)	568	624
St. Mary, Islington (*Vacant*)	479	543
St. Paul, Essex-road (*Rev. Alfred Havergal Shaw*)	669	556
St. Matthew, Essex-road (*Rev. U. Davies*)	350	269
St. John, Cleveland-road (*Rev. T. Lee*)	207	168
St. James, Prebend-square (*Rev. J. W. Horne*)	195	143
St. Peter, St. Peter-street (*Rev. A. Ewing*)	217	213
St. Stephen, Canonbury-road (*Rev. F. H. Nicholls*)	411	586
St. Luke, Hillmarton-road (*Rev. R. Glover*)	314	288
Emmanuel, Hornsey-road (*Rev. D. E. Holland*)	281	298
Holy Trinity, Cloudesley-square (*Rev. W. E. Haigh*)	549	683
St. Andrew, Thornhill-square (*Rev. A. J. Bridgman*)	474	483
All Saints, Caledonian-road (*Rev. A. Wardroper*)	194	264
St. David, Westbourne-road (*Rev. R. Hoare*)	92	126
St. Mary's Chapel of Ease (*Rev. W. Nelson Winn*)	520	750
St. James, Victoria-road (*Rev. E. A. Stuart*)	1262	1383
St. Matthias, Caledonian-road (*Rev. F. O. White*)	96	155
St. Michael, Bingfield-road (*Rev. R. Roe*)	124	157
St. Thomas, Hemington-road (*Rev. E. Brewer*)	232	350
St. Clement, Arundel-square (*Rev. J. K. Harrison*)	281	365
Congregational—	
Holloway Chapel, Camden-road (*Rev. J. M. Wilks*)	357	481
Offord-road (*Rev. J. Jones*)	243	215
Arundel-square Chapel (*Rev. H. Elwyn Thomas*)	397	572
Britannia-row (*Rev. M. Smith*)	159	429
Islington Congregational Church, River-street (*Rev. J. White*)	136	135
Caledonian-road (*Rev. N. McNeil*)	216	262
Barnsbury Chapel (*Rev. J. Ellis*)	209	267
Union Chapel (*Rev. Dr. Allon*)	900	736
Upper-street (*Rev. R. Berry*)	300	367
Crayford-road, Tufnell-park (*Rev. A. Verran*)	133	94
Junction-road, Upper Holloway (*Rev. W. J. Craig*)	145	206
New Court, Tollington-park (*Rev. J. Ossian Davies*)	1053	1326
Finsbury-park, Seven Sisters-road (*Rev. T. Eynon Davies*)	1021	1170

ISLINGTON. 41

	M.	E.
Congregational (*continued*)—		
Hare-court Chapel (*Rev. W. M. Statham*)	217	206
Highbury Quadrant (*Vacant*)	781	570
Maberley Chapel, Ball's Pond-road (*Vacant*)	41	64
Park Chapel, Crouch End (*Rev. A. Rowland*)	956	732
Baptist—		
Providence Chapel, Upper-street (*Rev. P. Reynolds*)	122	154
Belle Isle, Lower Holloway (*Mr. Joseph Benson*)	264	550
Salter's Hall Chapel, Baxter's road (*Rev. A. Bax*)	521	607
Salem Chapel, Wilton-square (*Rev. W. Flack*)	120	103
Cross-street Chapel (*Rev F. A. Jones*)	287	353
Camden-road Chapel (*Rev. G. Hawker*)	530	501
Grove-place, Upper Holloway (*Rev. J. R. Wood*)	960	1050
Hornsey-rise (*Rev. F. M. Smith*)	190	214
Zoar Chapel, Wedmore-street (*Rev. H. J. Boulton*)	50	57
Highbury-hill Chapel (*Rev. W. H. King*)	326	250
Highbury Vale (*Rev. J. Whitteridge*)	63	75
Gillespie-road, Highbury (*Various*)	13	16
Wesleyan—		
Liverpool-road (*Rev. R. P. Downes*)	362	490
Archway-road (*Rev. Joseph Dixon*)	507	447
Holly Park, Crouch-hill (*John Colwell*)	561	488
Hornsey-road (*Rev. J. T. L. Maggs*)	425	450
Highbury Church, Drayton Park (*Rev. Joseph Bush*)	290	250
Highbury Vale (*Rev. W. C. Bourne*)	11	33
Mildmay Park (*Rev. W. F. Slater*)	329	492
Welsh Calvinistic Methodist—		
Wilton-square	128	227
Sussex-road	113	228
Primitive Methodist—		
South-street, New North-road (*Rev. Thomas Guttery*)	92	162
Gillespie Road, Highbury (*Various*)	146	160
Caledonian-road (*Rev. George B. Gleghorn*)	205	253
Anatola-road (*Rev. H. J. Taylor*)	140	167
Durham-road (*Rev. Thomas Guttery*)	128	132
Methodist New Connexion—		
Packington-street (*Rev. Joseph Stark*)	165	171
United Methodist Free Church—		
Charlotte-street (*Rev. Thomas Foster*)	175	283
Presbyterian—		
Holly Park, Crouch-hill (*Rev. Dr. Murphy*)	420	306
Park Church, Grosvenor-road (*Rev. Dr. Edmond*)	611	444
Trinity Church, Canonbury (*Rev. G. Wilson*)	107	132
Colebrooke-row (*Rev. Dr. Davidson*)	610	550

Scotch Church—
	M.	E.
Caledonian Church (*Rev. J. S. Forsyth*)	173	196

Friends—
Mercers-road (*Various*)	87	41

Catholic Apostolic—
Duncan-street, Islington (*Mr. Hamilton*)	169	a213
Gloucester-road, Holloway (*Various*)	130	106

Unitarian—
Unity Church, Upper-street (*Rev. T. W. Freckelton*)	128	173
Highgate-hill (*Rev. Robert Spears*)	127	194

Christadelphian—
Wellington Hall, Upper-street (*Various*)	69	56
Islington-green (*Various*)	75	80

New Jerusalem Church—
Devonshire-street, Islington (*Rev. W. O'Mant*)	41	—
Camden-road (*Rev. Dr. Tafel*)	179	275

German Evangelical—
Fowler-road, Islington (*Rev. T. Kübler*)	90	78

Sandemanian—
Barnsbury Meeting House (*Various*)	98	—

Undenominational—
Aged Pilgrims' Asylum, Hornsey-rise	—	a75

Jews—
Dutch and Polish Synagogue, Poet's-road	374	—
North London Synagogue (*Rev. Julius Ab. Gouldstein*)	60	—

Workhouse—
Workhouse Chapel, St. John's-road (*Rev. E. J. Barnes.*)	359	247
St. Mary's Workhouse (*Rev. J. Kahn*)	231	92
Holloway Prison (*Rev. G. Plaford*)	485	—

Roman Catholic—
Church of the Sacred Heart (*Rev. Wm. Ignatius Dolan.*)	228	248
St. John the Evangelist (*Rev. Leopold Pycke*)	435	478
St. Joseph's Retreat, Highgate-hill (*Rev. Vincent Grogan.*)	506	566
Holloway Prison (*Rev. Thomas Carey*)	88	—

CHELSEA.

	M.	F.
Church of England—		
St. John, Harrow-road (*Rev. A. G. Pemberton*)	338	161
St. Jude, Kensal-green (*Rev. S. Bott*)	272	332
St. John, Ashburnham-road (*Rev. J. Shaw*)	356	448
Christ Church, Paradise-street (*Rev. G. S. Whitlock*)	243	188
Park Chapel, Park-walk (*Rev. Dr. Bennett*)	576	511
Old Church, Church-street (*Rev. R. H. Davies*)	359	680
St. Mark's College Church (*Rev. J. G. Cromwell*)	291	206
Holy Trinity, Sloane-street (*Rev. R. Eyton*)	885	523
St. Matthew, Walton-street (*Various*)	113	305
St. Saviour, Walton-street (*Rev. Dr. Strickland*)	312	229
St. Simon Zelotes, Moore-street (*Rev. A. J. Myers*)	286	274
St. Luke, Robert-street (*Rev. A. G. W. Blunt*)	689	1762
St. Jude, Turk's-road (*Rev. W. H. Dalton*)	197	167
Congregational—		
Markham-square (*Rev. J. L. Forster*)	509	890
Edith-grove, Fulham-road (*Vacant*)	303	338
Ashburnham, Uverdale-road (*Vacant*)	175	137
Radnor Chapel (Welsh) (*Rev. J. Rowlands*)	56	106
Baptist—		
Lower Sloane-street (*Rev. W. H. J. Page*)	293	213
Wesleyan—		
Kensal Town (*Rev. Thomas Hind*)	143	120
Justice-walk (*Rev. J. J. Brown*)	93	63
Sloane-terrace (*Rev. W. Brunyate*)	256	304
United Methodist Free Church—		
Middle-row, Kensal Town (*Rev. C. Tregowing*)	60	76
College-place (*Rev. J. Hocking*)	32	29
Marlborough-street (*Rev. J. Roberts*)	82	96
Primitive Methodist—		
Kilburn-lane (*Rev. G. Shapcott*)	264	175
Presbyterian—		
St. Columba, Pont-street (*Rev. D. Macleod*)	460	418
Undenominational—		
Wycliffe Union Tabernacle (*Various*)	160	600
Disciples of Christ—		
College-street, Fulham-road (*Various*)	96	119
Catholic Apostolic—		
College-street (*Rev. Richard Thomas Roskilly*)	168	120

Roman Catholic— | M. | E.
St. Mary, Cadogan-terrace (*Rev. J. L. Patterson*) | — | 346

Workhouses, Hospitals, etc.—
Workhouse Chapel, Arthur-street (*Rev. J. F. Downes*) 450 . —
Royal Military Asylum Chapel (*Rev. E. H. Godwin*) . 572 . 418
Royal Hospital Chapel (*Rev. S. Clark*) . . 330 . 200

LEWISHAM.

COMPRISING THE SUB-DISTRICTS OF ELTHAM, LEE, LEWISHAM VILLAGE, AND SYDENHAM.

Church of England—

	M.	E.
St. Margaret, Lee-terrace (*Rev. F. H. Law*)	816	517
Holy Trinity, Lee (*Rev. B. W. Bucke*)	695	730
St. Paul, Forest-hill	840	907
Christ Church, Forest-hill (*Rev. G. J. Jones*)	533	614
St. Michael, Sydenham (*Rev. H. R. Wakefield*)	170	135
St. Saviour, Brockley-hill (*Rev. W. L. Rosenthal*)	446	296
St. Bartholomew, Upper Sydenham (*Rev. H. W. Yeatman.*)	797	482
St. Mary, Lewisham (*Hon. and Rev. A. Legge*)	776	612
Boone Alms House Chapel, Lee (*Rev. F. W. Law*)	145	107
St. John, Lewisham High-road (*Rev. E. J. Hone*)	736	854
Christ Church, Sydenham (*Rev. G. J. Jones*)	251	337
Trinity Church, Sydenham-park (*Rev. H. Stevens*)	741	413
St. George, Catford (*Rev. C. N. Williams*)	423	389
St. Cyprian, Brockley (*Hon. and Rev. A. Legge*)	476	296
St. Philip, Sydenham (*Rev. J. G. Holmes*)	445	465
St. Matthew, Sydenham	324	269
St. Augustine, Honor Oak-park (*Rev. J. H. Morgan*)	336	249
Church of Transfiguration, Lewisham (*Rev. P. F. Tindall.*)	284	575
St. Stephen, Lewisham (*Rev. R. R. Bristowe*)	565	757
Christ Church, Shooter's-hill (*Rev. J. S. Masters*)	135	125
St. Andrew, Mottingham (*Rev. G. B. P. Viner*)	92	84
St. Peter, Eltham (*Rev. R. J. Simpson*)	436	297
St. John, Eltham (*Rev. W. J. Sowerby*)	340	284
Holy Trinity, Eltham (*Rev. T. N. Rowsell*)	274	267
Good Shepherd, Lee (*Rev. L. A. Smith*)	396	239
St. Mildred, Lee (*Rev. F. W. Helder*)	495	281
Christ Church, Lee-park (*Rev. W. F. Sinis*)	586	320
All Saints, Blackheath (*Rev E. S. Randolph*)	448	249
Church of Ascension, Blackheath (*Rev. W. A. Moberly*)	294	232
South End Chapel (*Rev. H. E. Bicknell*)	141	93
St. Mark, College-park (*Rev. T. J. West*)	479	590

LEWISHAM.

	M.	*F.*
Congregational—		
Lewisham Village (*Rev. J. M. Jones*)	754	492
Algernon-road, Lewisham (*Rev. J. Woodhouse*)	207	215
Blackheath Congregational Church (*Rev. C. Wilson*)	628	506
Burnt Ash-lane, Lee (*Rev. G. Crutchley*)	324	192
Eltham Congregational Church (*Rev. E. J. Penfold*)	135	133
Queen's-road, Forest-hill (*Rev. J. Bartlett*)	83	116
The Grove, Sydenham (*Rev. J. S. Hall*)	35	218
Stanstead-road, Catford-bridge (*Rev. S. T. Williams*)	42	124
Rushey-green, Catford (*Various*)	28	42
Baptist—		
Dartmouth-road, Forest-hill (*Rev. J. C. Foster*)	183	170
Shooter's-hill (*Rev. R. E. Chettleborough*)	157	160
Dacre-park, Lee (*Rev. W. R. Dexter*)	110	85
High-road, Lee (*Rev. J. Foston*)	278	130
Burnt Ash, Bromley-road	94	104
Catford-hill (*Rev. T. Greenwood*)	205	278
College-park, Lewisham (*Rev. W. Hazleton*)	77	74
Wesleyan—		
College-park, Lewisham (*Rev. John Jackson*)	321	300
High-street, Sydenham (*Rev. Thomas Brookes*)	385	420
Wildfell-road, Catford (*Rev. John Jackson*)	86	95
Bennett-park, Blackheath (*Rev. John Brash*)	250	180
Mottingham (*Rev. W. D. Sargeant*)	43	47
Methodist New Connexion—		
Trinity Church, Forest-hill (*Rev. J. E. Radcliffe*)	134	141
Primitive Methodist—		
Stanstead-road, Forest-hill (*Rev. William Wray*)	98	136
Presbyterian—		
Vanbrugh-park Church, Blackheath	127	95
St. John, Sydenham	375	257
Bible Christian—		
High-road, Lee (*Rev. Dr. J. O. Keen*)	175	104
Stanstead-road, Forest-hill (*Rev. John Gammon*)	145	211
Park-place Chapel (*Rev. Dr. J. O. Keen*)	29	40
High-road, Lee (*Rev. John Gammon*)	203	320
German Evangelical—		
Dacre-road, Forest-hill	109	—
Roman Catholic—		
Our Lady, Sydenham (*Rev. Wm. E. Addis*)	159	93
Our Lady, Blackheath (*Rev. F. Ford*)	267	158
Workhouse—		
Lewisham Workhouse	—	*a*136

GREENWICH.

COMPRISING THE SUB-DISTRICTS OF ST. PAUL, DEPTFORD; ST. NICHOLAS, DEPTFORD; GREENWICH.

Church of England—

	M.	E.
St. Andrew, Blackwall-lane (*Rev. J. Kyle*)	69	91
St. John, Blackheath (*Rev. J. W. Marshall*)	333	319
All Saints, Hatcham Park (*Rev. R. G. Smith*)	1221	1412
St. James, Hatcham (*Rev. S. A. Selwyn*)	586	994
St. Peter, Wickham-road, Brockley (*Rev. J. H. Titcombe.*)	1092	935
St. John, Deptford (*Rev. E. J. Hone*)	889	885
St. Nicholas, Deptford-green (*Rev. J. M. Vaughan*)	155	151
Christ Church, Deptford (*Rev. R. Pratt*)	110	194
St. Luke, Deptford (*Rev. J. Malcolmson*)	263	185
St. Paul, Deptford (*Rev. H. G. Gundy*)	231	368
St. Mary, Greenwich (*Rev. B. Lambert*)	249	297
Christ Church, Greenwich (*Rev. D. Reith*)	475	534
Holy Trinity, Blackheath-hill (*Rev. C. H. Simpkinson*)	489	480
St. Alphage, Greenwich (*Rev. B. Lambert*)	849	616
St. Paul, Greenwich (*Rev. A. Love*)	354	574
St. Peter, Greenwich (*Rev. F. S. Clark*)	113	156

Congregational—

	M.	E.
Lewisham High-road (*Rev. I. M. Wright*)	1250	972
Greenwich-road (*Rev. G Norton*)	232	163
Maze-hill Chapel (*Rev. E. H. Higgins*)	343	298
High-street, Deptford (*Rev. S. S. Read*)	306	381

Baptist—

	M.	E.
Octavius-street, Deptford (*Rev. D. Honour*)	276	536
Midway-place, Deptford-road (*Rev. F. W. Milledge*)	173	230
Zion Chapel, New Cross-road (*Rev. J. S. Anderson*)	326	400
Devonshire-road	262	336
Brockley-road, New Cross (*Rev. J. T. Wigner*)	615	404
Lewisham-road (*Rev. A. C. Gray*)	272	284
South-street, Greenwich (*Rev. C. Spurgeon*)	545	549

Wesleyan—

	M.	E.
Woolwich-road (*Rev. George Boggis*)	164	178
Brockley-road, Brockley (*Rev. John Wright*)	512	526
London-street, Greenwich (*Rev. T. Fletcher*)	346	423
French-fields, Deptford (*Rev. John Tucker*)	31	64
High-street, Deptford (*Rev. George Boggis*)	202	164

WOOLWICH. 47

	M.	F.
Wesleyan (*continued*)—		
New Cross (*Rev. John Wright*)	656	540
Morden Wharf (*Rev. T. Fletcher*)	5	6
Trafalgar-road (*Rev. S. Tucker*)	210	194
Methodist New Connexion—		
Victoria Chapel, Grove-street (*Various*)	134	115
United Methodist Free Church—		
Brunswick Church, Deptford (*Rev. H. Codling*)	109	148
Primitive Methodist—		
Napier-street, Deptford (*Rev. James W. Coad*)	29	55
Presbyterian—		
Brockley Presbyterian Church (*Rev. H. McIntosh*)	307	407
St. Mark, Greenwich (*Rev. G. Elder*)	247	222
Friends—		
Meeting-house, Deptford (*Various*)	13	110
Unitarian—		
Church-street, Deptford (*Rev. M. C. Gascoigne*)	33	61
Roman Catholic—		
Church of the Assumption (*Rev. M. P. Faunan*)	430	457
St. Joseph (*Rev. A. N. Boone*)	176	159
Our Lady (*Rev. M. C. O'Halloran*)	298	173
Workhouses, etc.—		
Greenwich Workhouse Chapel	301	219
East Greenwich Workhouse	167	106
Royal Naval School, New Cross	130	126
Seamen's Hospital Chapel	77	38
Royal Hospital Chapel	876	—

WOOLWICH.

COMPRISING THE SUB-DISTRICTS OF CHARLTON, WOOLWICH, AND PLUMSTEAD.

	M.	F.
Church of England—		
St. John, North Woolwich (*Rev. A. D. Piper*)	154	330
Holy Trinity, Woolwich (*Rev. Joseph Jordan*)	500	800
St. James, Plumstead (*Rev. S. Henning*)	429	472
St. George, Woolwich-common (*Rev. E. B. B. Kitson*)	1980	492
All Saints, Shooter's-hill (*Rev. T. V. Williams*)	427	422
St. Nicholas, Plumstead (*Rev. J. McAllister*)	251	188
St. John, Wellington-street (*Rev. J. O. Bent*)	321	365
Royal Arsenal Chapel (*Rev. C. A. Berry*)	79	81
Morden College Chapel	70	45
St. James, Blackheath	715	532
St. Germains, Blackheath (*Rev. R. H. Robinson*)	286	326

Church of England (continued)—

	M.	E.
St. Thomas, Old Charlton (*Rev. A. Morris*)	220	173
St. Michael, Blackheath-park (*Rev. B. Baring-Gould*)	459	344
St. Luke, Old Charlton (*Rev. C. Swainson*)	135	185
St. Michael, Woolwich (*Rev. H. R. Baker*)	201	416
St. Margaret, Plumstead (*Rev. J. McAllister*)	285	226
St. Paul, Old Charlton (*Rev. C. Witherby*)	470	381
St. Mary, Church-street (*Rev. S. G. Scott*)	325	750

Congregational—

Rectory-place (*Rev. A. J. Viner*)	334	335

Baptist—

Union Church, Plumstead	78	106
Conduit-road, Plumstead (*Rev. C. W. Townsend*)	116	157
Queen-street (*Rev. T. Jones*)	149	288
Elm-street, Plumstead	101	225
Enon Chapel, High-street (*Rev. W. K. Squirrell*)	206	208
Parson's-hill (*Rev. J. Wilson*)	413	711
Joseph-street, Charlton (*Various*)	57	96
Plumstead Tabernacle (*Various*)	58	64
Carmel Chapel, Anglesea-road (*Rev. B. B. Wale*)	130	200

Wesleyan—

Plumstead (*Rev. J. R. Hewitson*)	210	168
Shooter's-hill (*Rev. E. P. Lowrie*)	88	118
William-street (*Rev. F. R. Bell*)	475	399
Charlton-street (*Rev. J. Hugill*)	143	57
Plumstead Common-road (*Rev. J. R. Hewitson*)	452	539

United Methodist Free Church—

Beresford-street, Woolwich (*Rev. J. J. Layland*)	62	61
Crescent-road, Plumstead (*Rev. J. J. Layland*)	100	120

Primitive Methodist—

Robert-street, Plumstead (*Rev. Josiah Turley*)	326	321
Eglinton-road, Plumstead (*Rev. A. Jones*)	63	75
Zoar Chapel, Upper Market-street (*Rev. John Phillips*)	51	47

Presbyterian—

St. Andrew, Anglesea-road (*Rev. J. A. Rentoul*)	267	377
New-road, Woolwich (*Rev. W. Raitt*)	298	784

Believers—

Anglesea-hill (*Various*)	66	46
Nightingale-vale (*Various*)	154	382
Inverness-place (*Various*)	97	163

Roman Catholic—

St. Peter, New-road, Woolwich (*Rev. Jeremiah Cotter*)	787	805

Workhouse—

Plumstead Workhouse Chapel	150	160

SUMMARY OF RETURNS.

CITY OF LONDON—Population, 1881, 51,439.

	APPROXIMATE ACCOMMODATION	ATTENDANCE: MORNING	EVENING	TOTAL
Episcopal	35,000	9,456	10,694	20,150
Nonconformist	13,500	3,211	4,687	7,898
Roman Catholic	2,000	1,156	1,157	2,313
Jews	2,900	1,349	1,349	2,698
Hospitals	—	175	107	282

ST. GILES-IN-THE-FIELDS.—Population, 1881, 45,382.

Episcopal	6,200	1,646	2,068	3,714
Nonconformist	7,200	1,549	1,796	3,345
Roman Catholic	—	164	319	483

WESTMINSTER.—Population, 1881, 46,549.

Episcopal	6,000	2,702	2,791	5,493
Nonconformist	3,250	838	987	1,825
Roman Catholic	2,600	1,132	1,910	3,042
Jews	450	88	9	97
Workhouse	—	160	180	340

MARYLEBONE.—Population, 1881, 154,910.

Episcopal	30,000	13,679	13,647	27,326
Nonconformist	17,500	5,775	5,838	11,613
Roman Catholic	2,800	2,968	2,449	5,417
Jews	3,100	471	84	555
Greek Church	200	20	—	20
Workhouse	—	379	367	746

ST. GEORGE, HANOVER SQUARE.—Population, 1881, 149,748.

Episcopal	39,500	20,541	16,648	37,189
Nonconformist	12,250	3,118	3,176	6,294
Roman Catholic	2,600	1,012	971	1,983
Hospitals	—	137	40	177

HOLBORN.—Population, 1881, 151,835.

Episcopal	18,500	5,383	5,168	10,551
Nonconformist	17,000	3,814	5,113	8,837
Roman Catholic	3,700	475	485	960

THE RELIGIOUS CENSUS OF LONDON.

STRAND.—Population, 1881, 33,582.

	Approximate Accommodation.	Attendance: Morning	Evening	Total
Episcopal	6,500	1,229	1,828	3,057
Nonconformist	3,500	375	284	659
Roman Catholic	—	225	252	477
Jews	200	31	24	55

CAMBERWELL.—Population, 1881, 186,593.

Episcopal	21,500	13,017	13,528	26,545
Nonconformist	19,500	11,257	12,586	23,843
Roman Catholic	1,000	475	573	1,048
Workhouses and Hospitals	—	444	340	784

LAMBETH.—Population, 1881, 253,699.

Episcopal	46,000	17,984	19,086	37,070
Nonconformist	36,250	18,662	22,553	41,215
Roman Catholic	—	893	886	1,779
Hospitals and Workhouses	—	1,073	497	1,570

ST. SAVIOUR, SOUTHWARK.—Population, 1881, 195,164.

Episcopal	23,000	6,624	8,475	15,099
Nonconformist	18,000	4,805	6,339	11,144
Roman Catholic	3,000	2,273	2,634	4,907
Jews	400	55	14	69

ST. OLAVE, SOUTHWARK.—Population, 1881, 134,632.

Episcopal	15,500	3,224	4,026	7,350
Nonconformist	11,000	3,704	5,982	9,686
Roman Catholic	1,800	537	880	1,417
Hospital	—	126	86	212

SHOREDITCH.—Population, 1881, 126,591.

Episcopal	17,500	4,207	5,489	9,696
Nonconformist	7,500	1,352	1,976	3,328
Roman Catholic	350	132	194	326
Workhouse	—	160	120	280

BETHNAL GREEN.—Population, 1881, 126,961.

Episcopal	14,000	3,025	4,314	7,339
Nonconformist	11,000	4,260	5,665	9,925

WHITECHAPEL.—Population, 1881, 71,363.

Episcopal	9,000	1,987	2,359	4,346
Nonconformist	6,500	1,080	1,120	2,200
Roman Catholic	1,700	1,139	880	2,019
Hospital	—	146	127	273

SUMMARY OF RETURNS.

MILE END OLD TOWN.—Population, 1881, 105,613.

	Approximate Accommodation.	Attendance: Morning	Evening	Total
Episcopal	8,500	2,529	2,762	5,291
Nonconformist	11,500	4,704	5,941	10,645
Roman Catholic	700	541	606	1,147

STEPNEY.—Population, 1881, 58,543.

Episcopal	7,000	2,417	3,177	5,594
Nonconformist	3,000	673	949	1,622
Roman Catholic	1,000	424	156	580

ST. GEORGE-IN-THE-EAST.—Population, 1881, 47,157.

Episcopal	5,000	1,029	1,316	2,345
Nonconformist	3,500	1,116	1,364	2,480
Roman Catholic	650	325	475	800

POPLAR.—Population, 1881, 156,510.

Episcopal	14,500	5,091	6,399	11,490
Nonconformist	18,500	6,596	8,952	15,548
Roman Catholic	1,900	588	984	1,572
Workhouses, etc.	—	587	275	862

HACKNEY.—Population, 1881, 186,462.

Episcopal	25,250	16,487	15,722	32,209
Nonconformist	34,500	15,971	15,430	31,407
Roman Catholic	1,350	958	843	1,801

ST. PANCRAS.—Population, 1881, 236,258.

Episcopal	34,500	12,430	14,408	26,838
Nonconformist	27,250	12,645	13,655	26,300
Roman Catholic	2,600	1,181	1,473	2,654
Workhouses, etc.	—	1,111	290	1,401

HAMPSTEAD.—Population, 1881, 45,452.

Episcopal	11,000	7,970	6,122	14,092
Nonconformist	6,500	3,326	3,196	6,522
Roman Catholic	750	426	268	604
Workhouse	—	—	80	80

KENSINGTON.—Population, 1881, 162,924.

Episcopal	57,500	35,272	28,167	63,439
Nonconformist	25,250	9,246	11,856	21,102
Roman Catholic	7,000	3,780	4,748	8,528
Greek Church	700	179	—	179
Jews	1,450	422	—	422
Workhouses, Hospitals, etc	—	1,290	794	2,084

FULHAM.—Population, 1881, 114,839.

	Approximate Accommodation	Attendance: Morning	Evening	Total
Episcopal	15,500	9,024	7,983	17,017
Nonconformist	11,350	3,754	3,451	7,205
Roman Catholic	1,400	579	505	1,084

WANDSWORTH.—Population, 1881, 210,434.

Episcopal	27,500	24,747	20,716	45,463
Nonconformist	17,500	12,025	11,698	23,723
Roman Catholic	3,500	1,333	1,235	2,568
Workhouses, etc.	—	2,444	2,344	4,788

ISLINGTON.—Population, 1881, 282,865.

Episcopal	39,500	15,642	15,799	31,441
Nonconformist	39,000	17,736	20,484	38,220
Roman Catholic	1,750	1,029	1,044	2,073
Jews	650	374	60	434
Workhouses, etc.	—	1,075	339	1,414

CHELSEA.—Population, 1881, 88,128.

Episcopal	14,500	4,917	5,786	10,703
Nonconformist	7,500	3,150	3,790	6,940
Roman Catholic	600	—	346	346
Workhouses, Hospitals, etc.	—	1,352	618	1,970

LEWISHAM.—Population, 1881, 73,327.

Episcopal	20,500	13,915	12,065	25,980
Nonconformist	13,250	6,320	5,475	11,795
Roman Catholic	400	426	251	677
Workhouse	—	—	136	136

GREENWICH.—Population, 1881, 131,233.

Episcopal	18,000	6,678	7,591	14,269
Nonconformist	16,000	5,679	5,037	10,716
Roman Catholic	2,250	904	689	11,593
Hospitals, Workhouses, etc.	—	1,551	489	2,040

WOOLWICH.—Population, 1881, 80,825.

Episcopal	14,500	7,600	6,087	13,687
Nonconformist	11,500	4,444	6,047	10,491
Roman Catholic	800	787	805	1,592
Workhouses	—	150	160	310

	Other Me[tho]lic.			Jews.			Greek Church.	Hospitals, Work-houses, etc.	
	Approx. Accom.	At[tendan]ce.	Approx. Accom.	Attendance.					
[E]ven.		Morn. [E]ven.		Morn.	Even.	Morn. only.		Morn.	Even.
—	—	— 1,157	2,900	1,349	1,349	—		175	107
504	—	— 319	—	—	—	—		—	—
60	—	— 1,910	450	88	9	—		160	180
1797	750	19 2,449	3,100	471	84	20		379	367
5003	950	23 971	—	—	—	—		137	40
1183	—	— 485	—	—	—	—		—	—
—	—	— 252	200	31	24	—		—	—
1074	1,275	36 573	—	—	—	—		444	340
1131	1,700	83 886	—	—	—	—		1,073	497
5964	2,625	49 1,634	400	55	14	—		—	—
5851	2,350	59 880	—	—	—	—		126	86
5425	1,375	22 194	—	—	—	—		160	120
1915	400	8 —	—	—	—	—		—	—
1109	900	2 880	—	—	—	—		146	129
2505	1,500	24 606	—	—	—	—		—	—
5335	400	20 15	—	—	—	—		—	—
5463	900	17 475	—	—	—	—		—	—
1214	4,025	1,36 984	—	—	—	—		587	275
1720	2,075	82 843	—	—	—	—		142	124
5759	700	31 1,473	—	—	—	—		1,111	240
1697	—	— 268	—	—	—	—		—	80
1354	1,100	31 1,748	1,450	422	—	179		1,290	794
1685	1,000	58 505	—	—	—	—		—	—
1685	2,750	1,191 1,235	—	—	—	—		2,444	2,344
1182	2,575	1,055 1,292	650	434	—	—		1,075	339
0487	1,800	438 346	—	—	—	—		1,342	618
1042	750	23 251	—	—	—	—		—	136
0095	625	27 689	—	—	—	—		1,551	489
1281	1,850	602 802	—	—	—	—		150	160
1538	34,375	11,706 8,225	9,150	2,850	1,480	199		12,492	7,465

MISSION HALLS OF LONDON.

SUMMARY.

Denomination.	Approximate Accommodation.	Morning.	Afternoon.	Evening.	Total.
Church of England	40,516	6,027	4,318	15,751	26,096
Congregational	25,517	1,339	1,948	11,341	14,628
Baptist	21,198	3,835	2,375	10,415	16,625
Wesleyan Methodist	15,350	2,868	2,132	8,093	13,093
Primitive Methodist	710	144	36	204	384
Presbyterian	4,900	703	1,061	2,332	4,096
Brethren	4,050	1,309	185	2,053	3,547
Open Brethren	2,020	218	271	1,200	1,689
Friends	1,640	547	346	659	1,552
Unitarian	600	130	—	247	377
London City Mission	20,655	809	1,849	9,817	12,475
Undenominational	65,533	8,120	7,556	34,198	49,874
Mildmay Mission	3,570	—	519	1,447	1,966
Evangelistic Mission	3,540	663	338	2,134	3,135
Young Men's Christian Association.	6,095	14	573	3,481	4,068
Young Men's Christian Institute.	1,500	—	221	1,110	1,331
Christian Community	1,150	301	30	637	968
Church Army	3,800	22	98	1,046	1,166
Salvation Army	32,830	6,987	12,217	25,968	45,172
Miscellaneous	1,370	200	256	806	1,262
Total	256,544	34,236	36,329	132,939	203,504

NOTE.—Those Mission Halls which were closed on Census Sunday are not included in these lists.

KENSINGTON.

Comprising the Sub-Districts of St. Mary, Paddington; St. John, Paddington; Kensington Town; Brompton.

Missions.	Morning.	Afternoon.	Evening.	Accom.
Church of England—				
St. Peter's, 7, Chippenham-road (*Mr. W. H. Venables.*)	—	—	32	42
St. Ambrose, Clarendon-street	—	—	128	180
St. Matthew's School, Queen's-road (*Mr. W. Blake, L.C.M.*)	—	—	160	200
Onslow-square Church Room (*Rev. H. W. Webb-Peploe.*)	160	—	—	330
Onslow-square Church House Room (*Rev. H. W. Webb-Peploe.*)	—	—	155	160
St. Philip's, Kensington (*Rev. Arthur Baker.*)	—	—	—	40
St. Augustine's Church Mission (*Rev. R. R. Chope.*)	{ 8 a.m. 123 } { 11 a.m. 1030 }	—	—	1000
Christ Ch. Parish Hall, Faraday-rd. (*Rev. E. W. Clarke.*)	—	177	—	300
Harrow Mission, Latimer-road (*Rev. W. Law.*)	196	—	232	350
St. Mary Abbot's, Kensington-square (*Rev. Wm. Burnett.*)	—	—	55	100
St. James', St. Clement's-road (*Rev. R. McKenny.*)	—	—	150	160
St. Mark's, Bolton-street, Kensington (*Rev. Wm. E. Emmet.*)	—	—	103	—
St. Augustine's, Rudolf-road (*Lay Readers.*)	—	—	147	200
Magdalen Coffee Pal., Blechynden-st.	14	—	12	—
St. Barnabas, Warwick-road (*Rev. F. Smith.*)	—	—	100	130
Mission, Mary-place, Walmer-road (*Rev. A. E. Oldfield.*)	—	100	60	100
Walmer-road Firewood Brigade (*Rev. A. E. Oldfield.*)	—	—	50	—
Peckham-street, Ladbroke-grove (*Rev. H. Stapleton.*)	152	—	146	—
Congregational—				
Harrow-rd. Congregational Ch. Miss. (*Mr. D. S. Anderson.*)	—	900	—	—

MISSION HALLS—KENSINGTON.

Missions.	Morn- ing.	After- noon.	Even- ing.	Ac- com.
Baptist—				
Portobello-road, Notting-hill (*Rev. C. H. Spurgeon.*)	25	53	77	—
Wesleyan—				
Young Men's Chris. Assoc., Mall Hall (*Mr. Short, Sec. Y.M.C.A.*)	35	—	50	150
Presbyterian—				
Pembroke-road, Kilburn (*Mr. F. F. Darrock.*)	113	—	410	—
Mission Room, 256, Harrow-road (*Mr. H. R. Dewar.*)	—	—	55	60
Redfield-lane Mission, Earl's-court (*Mr. Macdermott.*)	—	—	70	150
Evangelistic—				
West Kensington Hall (*Mr. C. R. Hurditch.*)	65	—	287	—
Brethren—				
Moscow Hall, Moscow-road	45	—	40	100
Open Brethren—				
Kensal Hall, Kensal-road (*Mr. Bilke.*)	40	200	150	500
London City Mission—				
Boatman's Institution, Sale-street (*Mr. J. Connell.*)	60	30	93	—
Mission Room, 61, Amberley-road (*Mr. Alfred H. Learner.*)	—	—	75	80
Mission Room, Kilburn Park-road (*Mr. S. Wilson.*)	—	—	51	—
Jubilee Hall, Latimer-road (*Mr. E. J. Clark.*)	135	—	104	—
Clarendon Coffee Palace, Clarendon-rd. (*Mr. R. Mitchell.*)	—	—	15	—
Mission Hall, 15, Edge-st., Notting-hill (*Mr. S. Dyke.*)	28	—	96	150
Mission Room, 5, Edinburgh-road (*Mr. H. J. G. Harper.*)	—	88	47	60
Edge-street Mission, Notting-hill (*Mr. M. J. Lucas.*)	—	22	—	150
95, Tavistock-crescent, Notting-hill (*Mr. J. Robertson.*)	—	33	38	60

THE RELIGIOUS CENSUS OF LONDON.

Missions.	Morning.	Afternoon.	Evening.	Accom.
London City Mission *(continued)*—				
Schoolroom, Poplar-place, Bayswater (*Mr. Blake.*)	—	—	52	100
Mission Room, Fane-street. (*Mr. H. P. Blaxter.*)	—	—	31	—
Mission, 15, Appleford-road (*Mr. Bailey.*)	—	—	94	100
Mission Room, 9, Abingdon-road (*Mr. Joseph Baugh.*)	—	—	27	—
Undenominational—				
Queen's-park Hall, Harrow-road (*Dr. Hibberd.*)	30	150	200	—
6, St. Clement's-road, Notting-hill (*Mr. Spencer.*)	—	—	44	—
Temperance Hall, Oxford-rd., Kilburn (*Mr. Jupp.*)	—	—	81	—
Notting Dale Children's Mission (*Mr. E. Trickett.*)	—	—	95	—
Kensington Potteries Mission, Walmer-rd. (*Mr. E. Trickett.*)	—	—	242	—
Town Hall, Kensington (*Mr. J. Dawkins.*)	—	—	500	800
Norland Hall, Notting-hill (*Mr. Short.*)	—	—	54	—
Lock Hospital (*Mr. Charles Smallman.*)	—	—	55	—
Latimer-rd. Mission, Blechynden-st. (*Miss Gladstone, Hon. Sec.* / *Mr. Alf. Ireson, L.C.M.*)	84 / —	— / —	ch.98 / 40	250 / 250
Bible Mis. Room, 184A, Kenn. Park-rd. (*Miss C. Gurney.*)	15	52	62	150
People's Hall, 91, Latimer-road (*Mr. George Goss.*)	—	9	64	170
Golden Bells Coffee Pal., Notting-hill (*Lady Hope.*)	—	—	165	250
Bible Mis., 1, Walmer-rd., Notting-hill (*Mr. Groves, L.C.M.*)	—	—	77	100
Mission Hall, 15, Ranelagh-road	—	—	95	120
Gospel-room, Canterbury-rd., Kilburn.	20	20	28	—
North-end Mis. Hall, W. Kensington.	—	—	151	—
Metropolitan Music Hall, Edgeware-rd. (*Mr. C. Cook.*)	—	—	1892	2300
Hyde-park Hall, Stonecliffe-street (*Mr. C. Cook.*)	—	145	—	—
Cabmen's Mission, 2, Harrow-road	—	—	68	—
Earl-lane Mission Room, Sudbury (*Mr. J. Rixon.*)	—	—	19	—

MISSION HALLS—FULHAM.

Missions.	Morning.	Afternoon.	Evening.	Accom.
Salvation Army—				
Salvation Army Hall, Notting-hill (*Capt. J. Sperry.*)	7 a.m. 32 11 a.m. 118	270	560	—
Salv. Army Hall, Prince of Wales	7 a.m. 6 11 a.m. 36	90	108	—
Great Western Hall (*Capt. Clinton.*)	7 a.m. 46 10.30 a.m. 224	350	1083	—

FULHAM.

COMPRISING THE SUB-DISTRICTS OF ST. PETER, HAMMERSMITH; ST. PAUL, HAMMERSMITH; FULHAM.

Missions.	Morning.	Afternoon.	Evening.	Accom.
Church of England—				
St. Mary's Mission, 53, Melina-road (*Rev. J. Macnaught.*)	—	—	118	—
Baptist—				
Dawes-road, Fulham (*Various.*)	100	100	120	150
Wesleyan Methodist, German—				
Eustace-road, Walham-green (*Rev. J. Urech.*)	16	—	57	100
Primitive Methodist—				
Southerton-road, Fulham (*Rev. J. Sheale.*)	13	—	28	60
Salvation Army—				
Waterloo-street Hall (*Capt. Skinner.*)	7 a.m. 40 11 a.m. 200	360	1000	—
Salvation Army, Hounslow. (*Capt. J. Lyne.*)	7 a.m. 15 11 a.m. 37	120	470	—
Redmore-street Hall (*Lieut. Chatten.*)	7 a.m. 5 11 a.m. 20	40	53	—
Haydon Park-rd., Shepherd's Bush (*Capt. Hurd.*)	7 a.m. 7 11 a.m. 58	205	308	—
Young Men's Christian Association—				
Y.M.C.A., 27, Barclay-road. (*Mr. F. C. Wood.*)	14	46	50	60

Missions.	Morning.	Afternoon.	Evening.	Accom.
London City Mission—				
Greyhound-road Mission	60	140	80	100
(*Mr. Flew.*)				
Mansion House-street, Hammersmith.	8	—	123	180
(*Mr. J. Nelson.*)				
Crown-terrace, West Kensington	—	—	63	70
(*Mr. C. Elgar.*)				
177, Railway Arch, Hammersmith	—	—	250	320
(*Mr. T. O. Otway.*)				
Undenominational—				
Barclay Hall	48	—	150	—
Mission Hall, 391, Fulham-road	60	24	50	—
Park Hall, Shepherd's Bush	14	—	30	—
(*Mr. Page, Sec.*)				
Noel Hall, Fulham	—	—	50	—
(*Mr. R. Sinclair.*)				
Athenæum, Godolphin-road	—	109	317	450
(*Mr. F. A. Binder.*)				
Fulham Hall, 92, High-street	30	—	100	200
(*Mr. G. H. Gaze.*)				

CHELSEA.

Comprising the Sub-Districts of Chelsea, S.; Chelsea, N.W.; Chelsea, N.E.

Missions.	Morning.	Afternoon.	Evening.	Accom.
Church of England—				
St. Matthew's Mission, Walton-street.	76	—	168	—
(*Rev. H. W. Webb-Peploe.*)				
Cremorne Mission, Chelsea.	—	—	350	400
(*Rev. F. W. A. Wilkinson.*)				
Oakley Mission, Manor-street	60	—	199	—
(*Rev. H. W. Webb-Peploe.*)				
Church Army—				
St. Jude's Mission, Chelsea	{ 7.30 a.m. 4 } { 8.30 a.m. 10 }	33	65	—
(*Capt. T. Shepherd.*)				
Mission, 76, Kilburn-lane, Kensal-gn.	7.30 a.m. 8	35	45	—
(*Capt. Jessop.*)				
St. John's Hall, Blantyre-road	—	—	120	400
(*Capt. R. Wilson.*)				
Wesleyan—				
College-road, Kensal-green	11	—	36	100
(*Mr. H. Nicholls.*)				
Congregational—				
College-street Mission Hall	—	—	50	80
(*Rev. J. Lawson Forster.*)				

MISSION HALLS—CHELSEA.

Missions.	Morning.	Afternoon.	Evening.	Accom.
Presbyterian—				
Stuart Memorial Mission, Sloane-place (*Mr. H. B. Milne.*)	—	224	65 / 35	—
Open Brethren—				
Queen's Park Hall, Kilburn-lane. (*Mr. Bilke.*)	50	—	200	300
Salvation Army—				
Chelsea Salvation Army (*Capt H. Oxby.*)	7 a.m. 31 / 11 a.m. 182	210	500	—
London City Mission—				
Cornwall Mission, King's-road (*Mr. F. Borrough.*)	—	—	63	—
Star and Anchor Coffee Palace (*Mr. W. Stacy.*)	—	—	52	70
Redford Hall, Upper Manor-street (*Mr. A. Williams.*)	—	34	126	150
Temperance Hall, Pavilion-road. (*Mr. Tozer.*)	—	18	39	—
Kensal-road Mission (*Mr. G. Marchant.*)	—	121	60	200
Undenominational—				
Sydney Hall, Leader-street.	—	—	94	—
Tyndall House, 29, Whitehead's-grove	—	—	29	—
Mission Hall, Lackland-terrace	—	18	234	—
Mission Hall, 14, Sloane-terrace (*Mr. J. Goodchild.*)	—	24	22	—
Paradise Hall, Queen's-road (*Mr. Lorrimore.*)	—	40	49	—
Railway Mission Hall, Kensal-road	—	71	168	450
Chelsea Town Hall, King's-road.	—	74	250	—
Christian Mission, Queen's-road. (*Mr. A. Stalker.*)	53	130	98	—
Bethel Mission, Lower Sloane-street	—	—	36	—
Oxford-road Temperance Hall (*Mr. Jupp.*)	—	—	81	—
Gospel Room, Canterbury-road (*Mr. T. Luff.*)	—	—	29	—

ST. GEORGE, HANOVER SQUARE,.

Comprising the Sub-Districts of Hanover-square, Mayfair, Belgrave, St. John's, Westminster, and St. Margaret, Westminster.

Missions.	Morning.	Afternoon.	Evening.	Accom.
Church of England				
South Eaton-place Mission (Mr. Charles Hobbs.)	—	—	—	25
Westminster Town Hall (Father Ignatius; Rev. J. V. Smeadley.)	361	385	920	800
St. Stephen's Schools, Rochester-row. (Rev. J. Newlyn.)	—	—	170	—
St. Stephen's Mission, Rochester-row. (Rev. W. Sinclair.)	—	6	—	70
St. Andrew's Mission, Palace-street (Mr. T. R. Rutledge.)	—	—	75	100
Blue Ribbon Hall, Marsham-street (Rev. R. McMillar.)	—	—	40	150
Hanover Church Mission, Gilbert-st. (Mr. E. W. West.)	—	—	65	—
Congregational—				
Besborough Hall. (Mr. C. de Selincourt.)	83	—	456	400
Baptist—				
Ebury Mission, Pimlico-row (Mr. C. F. Allison.)	—	—	120	200
Evangelistic—				
Conference Hall, Eccleston-street (Lord Radstock.)	—	53	183	1000
Young Women's Christian Association—				
Y.W.C.A., 2, St. George's-road (Miss Maunsell.)	—	36	—	100
Salvation Army—				
Regent's Hall (Capt. Isaac Unsworthy.)	{7 a.m. 54} {11 a.m. 518}	833	2800	—
London City Mission—				
Mission, 188, Ebury-street, S.W. (Mr. R. Weaver, Jun.)	—	—	63	120
Christ Church Schools Mission. (Mr. R. Pugh.)	—	—	18	40
Pear-street Mission, Strutton-ground. (Mr. G. Owen.)	—	—	98	—
Mission, 76, Great Peter-street. (Mr J. Matthews.)	—	—	17	—
New Peter-st. Mission, Westminster. (Mr. J. Saunders.)	—	—	100	—

MISSION HALLS—WESTMINSTER.

Missions.	Morning.	Afternoon.	Evening.	Accom.
Undenominational—				
Bethel Mission, Brunswick-row. (*Mr. J. Richards.*)	—	—	{ 7 p.m. 70 { 8 p.m. 20	50
Westminster Hall, Regency-street	21	—	No service	250
One Tun Schools Mission, Old Pye-st. (*Mr. W. Geary, Manager.*)	—	—	72	—
Westminster Temp. Hall, Regency-st.	25	—	—	—
Rose and Crown Coffee Palace. (*Mr. Charles Heath.*)	—	—	36	120

WESTMINSTER.

Comprising the Sub-Districts of St. James', Westminster; St. Anne, Soho.

	Morning.	Afternoon.	Evening.	Accom.
Church of England—				
St. Margt's. Mission, Dartmouth Hall. (*Ven. Archdeacon Farrar.*)	—	100	100	180
Congregational—				
Mission Hall, 50, Lexington-street (*Mr. O. Cromwell.*)	—	—	60	150
Baptist—				
Bloomsbury Hall, Meard-street. (*Mr. Harrison.*)	210	—	331	700
Wesleyan West-Central Mission—				
St. James's Hall, Piccadilly (*Rev. Hugh Price Hughes.*)	878	1120	2405	2400
Young Men's Christian Association—				
Y.M.C.A. West Branch (*Mr. J. Pearse, Sec.*)	—	40	—	60
London City Mission—				
Italian Mission, 2, Frith-street, Soho. (*Mr. W. Boulnois.*)	—	—	21	35
Mission, 60, Frith street, Soho (*Mr. Pino.*)	—	80	70	120
Male Lock Hospital, Dean-street (*Mr. Pell.*)	—	20	20	—
Pall Mall Mission, 48, Lisle-street (*Mr. J. Bridge.*)	—	23	40	80
Undenominational—				
Aberdeen Schools, Foubert-place (*Miss M. Constance, Sec.*)	—	—	56	—
French Mission, 6, Frith-street (*Mr. J. F. Cantwell.*)	—	63	21	80

MARYLEBONE.

Comprising the Sub-Districts of All Souls; Cavendish-square; Rectory; St. Mary; Christchurch; St. John.

Missions.	Morn-ing.	After-noon.	Even-ing.	Ac-com.
Church of England—				
Welsh Church Mis., St. Mary's N. Sc. (*Mr. J. E. Davis, Sec.*)	—	—	64	—
Emmanuel Church Mission, North-st. (*Mr. J. Robson, Scripture R.*)	—	—	70	—
Gray's-yard Rag. Church and School (*Mr. Philip Gough.*)	120	—	570	440
Reeve Mission, East-street (*Rev. H. N. Sherbrook; Mr. A. J. Winter, L.C.M.*)	—	—	165	—
St. Thomas' Mis., James-st., Oxford-st. (*Rev. H. Geary.*)	—	—	37	—
All Souls' Church Home, Nassau-st. (*Rev. W. H. Chapman.*)	—	—	16	120
All Souls' Church Home, Nassau-st. (*Rev. W. R. Mowll.*)	—	—	62	—
St. Barnabas' Mission, 14, Bell-street. (*Capt. Baillie.*)	120	135	60	110
Church Army—				
St. Mary's Hall, Crawford-street (*Capt. Hotchkiss.*)	—	—	250	700
Congregational—				
St. John's Wood-terrace Schoolroom (*Mr. H. Tollet*)	—	—	80	130
Earl-street Mission, Lisson-grove (*Mr. Montague Holmes.*)	—	—	192	250
Baptist—				
Trinity Chapel, Devonsh.-mews, Inst. (*Rev. H. Trotman.*)	—	—	35	—
Workman's Hall, Henry-street, N.W. (*Rev. W. Stott.*)	—	—	180	200
Workman's Hall, Portland-town. (*Mr. A. Cutler.*)	40	200	200	220
Wesleyan—				
North Finchley Mission (*Mr. Easter.*)	50	—	100	200
Presbyterian—				
Bell-street Mission (*Dr. D. Fraser.*)	22	—	110	300

Missions.	Morn-ing.	After-noon.	Even-ing.	Accom.
Brethren—				
Meeting Room, 71, Welbeck-street	77	—	62	—
Open Brethren—				
Union Hall, Carlisle-st., Edgware-rd.	—	—	400	—
(*Mr. Robert Bilke.*)				
Prayer and Bible Mission—				
The Hall, 12, Bell-st., Edgware-road	—	45	130	—
(*Dr. Kirby.*)				
Evangelistic—				
Kilburn Hall, Kilburn-gate	255	65	603	750
(*Mr. C. Russell Hurditch.*)				
Christians—				
St. John's Rooms, St. John's-place	51	—	66	—
(*Mr. Hammond.*)				
Immersion Believers—				
Mission, 143, Marylebone-road	8	19	27	50
("*Elders.*")				
United Christian Society—				
New Prov. Hall, 347A, Edgware-rd.	101	106	90	160
(*Mr. Stephen Fowler.*)				
Young Men's Christian Association—				
Stafford Rooms, Edgware-road	—	125	115	—
(*Mr. Mills, Sec.*)				
Young Men's Christian Institute—				
Polytechnic, Regent-street	—	221	1110	1500
(*Mr. J. E. K. Studd.*)				
Young Women's Christian Association—				
Y.W.C.A., 17, Old Cavendish-street	—	—	95	130
(*Miss M. F. Ely.*)				
London City Mission—				
Mission, 95, Boston-place, Dorset-sq.	—	—	45	100
(*Rev. W. Hurdle; Dr. Stewart.*)				
Church-pl. Mission Hall, Paddington	—	—	54	—
(*Mr. James Lambourne.*)				
Mis., Townshend-cots., Portland-town	—	—	60	150
(*Mr. J. Powell.*)				
Cuthbert-st., Church-st., Edgware-rd.	—	17	67	100
(*Mr. George Reed.*)				
Portman Market Mission, Church-st.	51	—	112	—
Little Church-st., Mis., Edgware-road	—	—	180	—
(*Mr. Smith.*)				

Missions.	Morning.	Afternoon.	Evening.	Accom.
Salvation Army—				
Salvation Army, Kilburn (*Capt. A. Bell.*)	{ 7 a.m. 17 11 a.m. 75 } 91		261	—
Undenominational—				
Nutford Hall, Nutford-place (*Mr. Sage; Mr. Davies.*)	33	29	96	150
North-st. Domestic Mis., Lisson-grove (*Mr. Thomas Robinson.*)	—	—	63	100
Paddington Hall, Church-street	30	70	50	100
Home for W. Boys, 22, Dorchester-pl. (*Mr. H. Bristow Wallen.*)	—	—	22	—
St. James' Hall, George-st., Lisson-gr. (*Mr. Sprunt.*)	—	—	78	—

HAMPSTEAD.

	Morning.	Afternoon.	Evening.	Accom.
Church of England—				
St. Saviour's Mission, Fleet-road (*Rev. G. A. Herklots.*)	—	—	130	200
Memorial Hall, Hampstead (*Rev. G. F. Head.*)	—	—	250	300
North End Mission, Hampstead (*Rev. G. F. Head.*)	64	—	84	140
Church Army—				
Church Army, North Finchley (*Capt. John Willey.*)	—	30	97	—
Young Men's Christian Association—				
Y.M.C.A., Willoughby-road (*Mr. Arthur Welsh.*)	—	—	47	50
Salvation Army—				
Hampstead Salvation Army (*Capt. J. Burslem.*)	{ 7 a.m. 14 11 a.m. 50 } 120		160	—
London City Mission—				
Oak Village Gospel Hall, Gospel Oak (*Mr. R. Crewdson.*)	—	—	72	70

ST. PANCRAS.

COMPRISING THE SUB-DISTRICTS OF REGENT'S PARK, TOTTENHAM COURT, GRAY'S INN LANE, SOMERS TOWN, CAMDEN TOWN, KENTISH TOWN.

MISSION HALLS—ST. PANCRAS.

Missions.	Morning.	Afternoon.	Evening.	Accom.
Church of England—				
St. Andrew's, 137, Weedington-road	—	—	16	50
(*Mr. Dawson.*)				
Mission, Lancing-street	—	—	40	—
(*Mr. Flanders; Mr. Gibbs.*)				
St. Bede's, William-st., Albany-st.	24	—	204	250
(*Mr. H. U. Whelpton.*)				
St. Saviour's, 61, Warren-street	100	—	109	200
(*Messrs. H. G. Pinn; H. A. McLaren; C. Walker.*)				
St. Jude's Mission, King's-cross	—	—	18	120
(*Rev. J. M. Andrews.*)				
St. Jude's School, King's-cross	—	136	—	200
(*Rev. J. M. Andrews.*)				
Church Army—				
St. Mary's Mission, Polygon	—	—	33	—
(*Capt. Payne.*)				
Mis. House, C.A., 11, Manchester-st.	—	—	17	—
(*Capt. J. Culledge.*)				
Trinity Mission, 139, Cleveland-street	—	—	45	100
(*Canon Cadman, Vicar; Capt. H. Goldstone.*)				
St. Mark's Charlotte-st., Fitzroy-sq.	—	—	64	300
(*Canon Cadman, Vicar; Capt. H. Goldstone.*)				
Congregational—				
Lyndhurst Mission Hall	—	—	38	80
(*Mr. J. Howard Glover.*)				
Tolmers-sq., Ch. Inst., Drummond-st.	—	—	114	700
(*Mr. J. Denchfield.*)				
Mis. Cong. School, King's Cross-road	—	—	27	400
(*Mr. W. J. Howell.*)				
Whitfield Tab. Schools Mission	—	—	90	100
(*Mr. J. H. Skipper.*)				
Christchurch Mission, Somers-town	—	—	36	—
Grafton-terrace Mission, Malden-road	—	—	140	250
Baptist—				
Drummond-street Mission Hall	—	9	108	200
(*Mr. Brown.*)				
Wesleyan—				
Wesleyan Mission, Camden-street	147	345	290	500
(*Mr. W. C. Rose.*)				
Mis. Hall, Compton-st., St. Pancras	—	—	80	120
(*Rev. A. Clayton.*)				
Agincourt-road, Gospel-oak	155	—	148	400
(*Mr. Elmes.*)				

THE RELIGIOUS CENSUS OF LONDON.

Missions.	Morning.	Afternoon.	Evening.	Accom.
London City Mission—				
Mis. Hall, Cromer-st., Gray's-inn-road (*Mr. G. Bridge.*)	—	—	80	150
Mission, Arlington-rd., Camden-town (*Rev. J. C. Harrison.*)	—	—	25	40
Dickenson-st. Hall, Kentish-town (*Mr. C. Cox.*)	7.30 a.m. 80	160	330	350
Camden Hall, King-st., Camden-town (*Mr. J. Mills.*)	—	—	63	—
Cardington-street Mission, Euston (*Mr. F. P. Harris.*)	—	—	51	—
Southampton-rd. Mission, Kentish-tn. (*Mr. J. Stevens.*)	—	12	46	90
Haverstock Mission Hall, Grafton-ter. (*Mr. R. M. Darby.*)	—	—	140	250
North Hill Mission Hall, Highgate (*Mr. J. Grout.*)	—	—	38	100
Mis. Rm., 8, Harmood-st., Chk. Fm.-rd. (*Mr. George Green.*)	—	7	62	60
Camden Town Hall (*Mr. S. Lee.*)	—	—	14	—
Presbyterian—				
Marchmont Hall, Marchmont-street (*Mr. J. B. Thorburn.*)	10	31	—	—
King's-cross Theatre (*Rev. Z. B. Woffendale.*)	—	130	120	400
Mis. Hall, Leighton-rd. Kentish-town (*Rev. R. N. Thornton; Mr. W. R. Copeland, L.C.M.*)	—	—	215	250
Presbytern. Mis. Hall, Compton-place (*Mr. James Filkins, Miss.; Mr. John Coutts, Supt.*)	—	—	40	140
Mildmay Mission—				
Mission, 158, King's Cross-road (*Mr. J. E. Mathieson.*)	—	90	23	—
Evangelistic—				
Malden Hall, Malden-street (*Mr. C. R. Hurditch.*)	210	70	522	600
Undenominational—				
Grange Mis., 78, King's Cross-rd.	—	—	80	—
Gt. Northern Temp. Hall, Chenies-st.	—	—	50	—
Domestic, 4, Rhyl-st., Kentish-town (*Mr. J. Pollard; Mr. J. E. L. Pollard.*)	237	—	233	300
St. George's Hall, Regent-street (*Mr. S. Henry.*)	437	—	562	—

MISSION HALLS—ISLINGTON.

MISSIONS.	MORNING.	AFTERNOON.	EVENING.	ACCOM.
Undenominational (*continued*)—				
People's Gospel Mission, Retcar-st.	—	46	136	—
(*Mr. R. Avery, President.*)				
Aldenham Hall, Aldenham-street	—	—	51	100
(*Mr. S. C. Griffith.*)				
Cabmen's Mis. Hall, King's Cross	7.30 a.m. 11	15 Y.W.C.A. 28 „ 22	7 p.m. 55 8.30, 21	350
(*Mr. J. Dupee.*)				
Young Men's Christian Association—				
Y.M.C.A., 17, Camden-road	—	75	80	—
(*Mr. Walter Jervis, Sec.*)				
„ 91, Euston-rd., King's Cross	—	25	—	75
(*Mr. D. J. Lewis, Sec.*)				
Salvation Army—				
Salvation Army, Chalk Farm-road	7 a.m. 11 „	60 250	487 . 800	800
(*Capt. J. Keates.*)				
„ „ King's Cross	7 a.m. 11 „	23 195	209 . 220	300
(*Capt. Peck.*)				

ISLINGTON.

COMPRISING THE SUB-DISTRICTS OF UPPER HOLLOWAY, ISLINGTON, S.W., ISLINGTON, S.E., HIGHBURY.

	MORNING.	AFTERNOON.	EVENING.	ACCOM.
Church of England—				
Mission, Canal-road, King's Cross	—	—	41	200
St. Mary's Room, Hornsey	25	—	153	—
(*Rev. W. S. Lewis, Vicar.*)				
All Saints' Mission, Thornhill-road	—	70	43	—
(*Rev. A. Wardroper, Vicar.*)				
All Saints' Mission, Rupert-road	—	—	36	150
(*Mr. H. Hickin.*)				
St. James' Lecture Hall, Eden-grove	—	—	385	—
(*Mr. G. C. Williamson.*)				
St. John the Evangelist Mission	—	40	130	—
(*Rev. C. Ough.*)				
Archway, St. John's, Upper Holloway	75	—	74	—
(*Rev. A. G. Gristock.*)				
St. James' Mission, Britannia-row	—	292	102	450
(*Mr. W. T. Moore.*)				
St. Barnabas' Mission House	—	21	84	—
(*Rev. A. E. Whish, Vicar.*)				
St. Luke's Mission, West Holloway	—	—	51	300
(*Rev. R. Glover.*)				

MISSIONS.	Morning.	Afternoon.	Evening.	Accom.
Church of England (*continued*)—				
Bishop Wilson's Mem. Hall, Church-st.	—	19	100	400
(*Rev. W. H. Barlow: Mr. H. Smith, Warden.*)				
Rufford-row Mission, Essex-road	—	—	38	110
(*Students' Church Miss. Coll.*)				
Grafton Hall, Holloway	—	—	127	—
East-street, Gifford-street	200	500	225 50	—
(*Mr. W. Adams.*)				
Congregational—				
Metropolitan Benefit Society's Asylum	—	—	—	—
Gifford-Hall, Offord-road	—	821	548	700
(*Mr. B. Clark.*)				
Mission Hall, Blenheim-rd., Hornsey	—	—	149	450
(*Rev. E. Austin.*)				
Union Hall, Station-road, Highbury	—	—	90	280
(*Mr. G. B. File.*)				
Britannia-row Mission, N.	106	—	398	—
(*Mr. M. Smith.*)				
Holloway Hall	—	670	—	1000
Morton-road Mission Hall, N.	—	35	98	130
(*Mr. T. Chatterton, L.C.M.*)				
Myrtle-street Hall	—	—	140	200
(*Mr. J. J. Olding.*)				
Morton-road Mission, Essex-road / Station-road Hall, Highbury	—	—	309	420
(*Rev. Dr. Allon.*)				
Baptist—				
Blundell-st. Mission, Caledonian-road	120	—	140	250
(*Mr. J. M. Smith.*)				
Hercules-road Mission, Holloway	—	—	44	75
(*Mr. G. F. Dorrington.*)				
Highbury Hill Mission, Gillespie-road	—	—	36	50
(*Mr. J. Vanstone.*)				
St. Giles Christn. Mis., Caledonian-rd.	—	—	57	—
(*Mr. S. Hatton.*)				
Rupert-road	—	—	120	100
(*Mr. G. W. Foremen.*)				
Goodinge-road Mission Hall	—	—	113	120
(*Rev. G. Hawker; Mrs. Glover.*)				
Wesleyan Mission—				
Mission Day Schools, Drayton-park	—	—	50	—
(*Rev. C. F. Nightingale.*)				
Mission Hall, Windsor-st., Islington	25	—	61	—
Twyford Hall, Caledonian-road	45	—	160	200
(*Mr. F. A. Hyde.*)				
Mission Room, Gillespie-road	23	—	66	—

MISSION HALLS—ISLINGTON.

Missions.	Morn- ing.	After- noon.	Even- ing.	Ac- com.
London City Mission—				
Mildmay Cabman's Mission	80	—	70	—
(*Mr. John Crabb.*)				
North-hill Mission, Highgate	—	—	50	100
(*Mr. J. Grout.*)				
Essex-st. Mission Hall, Kingsland-rd.	—	—	63	—
(*Mr. R. Birkett.*)				
Mission Rm., Ingram-pl., Hornsey-rd.	—	—	70	100
(*Mr. E. Haynes.*)				
Mildmay Mission—				
Conference Hall, Mildmay	—	320	784	2500
(*Mr. J. E. Matheson.*)				
Ball's Pond-road Mission Hall	—	34	87	150
(*Mr. W. H. Gadsby.*)				
Undenominational—				
Agricultural Hall, Islington	—	1171	1626	3000
(*Rev. Dr. Thain Davidson.*)				
Rosemary Mis. Hall, Shepperton-road	—	—	16	—
Drovers' Hall, Cattle Market	—	—	90	300
Sermon-lane Mission, Liverpool-rd.	54	—	138	400
(*Mr. G. Fuller.*)				
Mission, Lennox-road, Finsbury-park	58	—	166	—
Mission Hall, 301, Holloway-road	19	25	45	70
(*Mr. H. Putterill.*)				
Cholmley Mission, 102, Archway-rd.	100	—	—	120
Institute Mis., Park-pl., Highbury-vale	—	60	34	—
Mission, Holmsdale-rd., New Southgate	16	—	294	—
Unsectarian—				
Gospel Hall, Highbury Corner	9	25	85	100
(*Mr. Ramsey.*)				
Mission, 134, Holloway-road	64	58	120	—
Brethren—				
Hampton Hall, Holloway	40	—	60	150
(*Mr. J. W. Burgess.*)				
309, Holloway-road	—	—	56	—
Open Brethren—				
Assembly Hall, Junction-road	72	71	180	220
(*Mr. F. Ferriman; Mr. C. F. Bilson.*)				
Young Men's Christian Association—				
Priory Hall, 198, Upper-street, N.	—	—	201	300
(*Mr. J. J. Atkinson.*)				
Finsbury-park Hall	—	—	798	800
(*Mr. R. A. Elvery.*)				

THE RELIGIOUS CENSUS OF LONDON.

MISSIONS.	MORN-ING.	AFTER-NOON.	EVEN-ING.	AC-COM.
Young Women's Christian Association—				
41, Pyrland-road, Canonbury	—	40	—	—
Salvation Army—				
Salv. Army Barracks, Milton-rd. (*Capt. Wells.*)	7 a.m. 31 / 11 „ 170	350	500	500
Hornsey-road, Holloway (*Capt. Clifton Bailey.*)	7 a.m. 42 / 11 „ 90	160	210	200
Holloway Salvation Army (*Capt. Wilner.*)	7 a.m. 21 / 10.30 230	465	800	750

HACKNEY.

COMPRISING THE SUB-DISTRICTS OF STOKE NEWINGTON, STAMFORD HILL, WEST HACKNEY, HACKNEY, SOUTH HACKNEY.

Church of England—

	MORN.	AFTER.	EVEN.	ACCOM.
St. Barnabas' Hall, High-st., Homerton (*Rev. F. R. Blatch, Vicar.*)	—	—	151	—
West Hackney Mission, Hindle-street	—	—	140	—
St. Paul's Mission, Duncan-street (*Rev. F. E. Ellerton.*)	38	144	81	120
Ada-street Church Mis. (St. Michael's) (*Mr. W. Vaughan.*)	—	—	43	80
Good Shepherd Mis., High-hill-ferry (*Messrs. Westfield and Wheeler.*)	154	—	118	150
Church Army, Hackney (*Capt. W. F. Elmes, C.A.*)	—	—	157	250
St. Mary's Mis., Church-st., Stoke New. (*Mr. J. A. Le Couteur.*)	160	20	130	150
Shacklewell-grn. Mission, Norfolk-rd.	—	46	53	70
Palestine-place Mission, Camb. Heath. (*Rev. J. B. Barraclough.*)	84	17	66	350
Church Room, The Grove, Hackney (*Rev. J. Beardale.*)	—	—	251	250
St. Faith's Hall, Londesboro'-road (*Rev. C. W. V. Pixell.*)	—	—	117	—
St. Luke's Mission, Kenton-road (*Mr. W. H. Bramwell.*)	—	175	160	—
St. John's Ch. Mis., Grove, Hackney (*Rev. A. Brook.*)	123	—	—	264
London Fields Mission, William-green (*Cottage meeting for the present.*)				

MISSION HALLS—HACKNEY.

Missions.	Morning.	Afternoon.	Evening.	Accom.
Church of England (*continued*)—				
King's Cross Mis., Cambridge Heath (*Rev. J. Allen.*)	97	—	152	—
Holy Trinity Mission, Lea-bridge	—	—	200	250
All Saints', Aden-grove, Green-lanes (*Mr. Alexander Mottram.*)	—	—	383	400
West Hackney Mission, Cleveland-st.	—	—	60	—
Congregational—				
Old Gravel Pit Mission, Hockley-st. (*Mr. J. Potter.*)	—	—	64	80
Kingsland Hall, Castle-st., Kingsland (*Mr. Felmingham, L.C.M.*)	—	—	108	120
Chapman-rd. Mission, Whitepost-lane (*Rev. J. Wood.*)	100	—	65	110
Morning-lane Mission, Hackney (*Mr. C. Palmer.*)	—	—	67	150
Glyn-road Mission, Clapton Park (*Mr. J. B. Uffen.*)	53	45	236	300
St. Ann's-road Mission (*Mr. Cook.*)	—	—	90	250
Sandford-lane Miss., Stoke Newington (*Mr. P. F. Holden.*)	—	—	116	100
Dove-row Mission, Goldsmith-row (*Mr. W. P. Cotsford.*)	—	—	83	120
Morley Hall, Hackney (*Mr. Sawell.*)	—	—	709	1500
Mission, Canal-road, Dalston (*Mr. Ashford.*)	—	—	43	70
Grove Mission Room, Brooksley-walk (*Rev. W. J. Woods.*)	—	—	156	400
Dunn-st. Mission, Shacklewell (*Mr. Hoon.*)	—	—	129	200
Well-street Mission, Hackney (*Mr. C. Edmond, Hon. Sec.*)	—	—	95	350
Adelphi Hall, Moye-st., Goldsmith-row (*Rev. R. B. Lander.*)	—	—	63	200
Baptist—				
Ann's-place Mission, Pritchard-road (*Mr. W. J. Hurry.*)	—	—	30	200
Combosa-road Mission, Hackney-wick (*Mr. Cadman.*)	95	—	130	—
Landfield-street, Rendlesham-road (*Mr. W. J. Way.*)	—	—	118	300

Missions.	Morn-ing.	After-noon.	Even-ing.	Ac. com.
Baptist (*continued*)—				
Clonbrook Hall, Clonbrook-road (*Mr. J. Wicks.*)	59	40	75	300
Wellington-rd. Mis., Stoke Newington (*Mr. C. R. W. Offen; Mr. C. Hart.*)	89	—	341	—
Waterloo Rooms, 2, Prout-rd., Clapton (*Mr. W. Kent.*)	—	—	82	60
Rupert-road (*Mr. S. W. Forman.*)	—	—	120	120
Wesleyan—				
People's Gospel Mis., 244, Hackney-rd. (*Mr. J. Potter.*)	10	12	65	—
Day Schoolroom Mission, Church-road (*Mr. W. H. Wilson.*)	108	—	170	250
Elgin-street Mis., 34, Hackney-wick (*Rev. D. Walters.*)	120	—	160	300
The Grove Mission, Hackney (*Mr. C. Little.*)	—	—	76	130
Church-road, Homerton (*Mr. H. Wilson.*)	114	—	182	250
Clapton-park Wesleyan Mission Hall (*Rev. G. Kenyon.*)	51	—	106	200
Matthias-road Mission (*Mr. J. Whiten.*)	30	—	150	250
Brethren—				
Clapton Hall, Stoke Newington	700	—	570	—
Primitive Methodist—				
Aveley-rd. Mission, Upper Clapton (*Mr. R. Giffen.*)	30	36	55	50
Undenominational—				
Evangel. Mis. Hall, High-st., Homerton (*Mr. J. J. Jones.*)	—	30	150	200
Hackney-rd. Missn. Hall, Union-cres. (*Mr. John Girling.*)	30	—	93	150
Marion-street Mission, Homerton (*Mr. J. Brett, Hon. Sec.*)	—	—	25	60
Cot. Mis., 18, Spencer-rd., Stoke New. (*Mr. E. A. Jackson, Hon. Sec.*)	—	—	32	—
John-st., Homerton, Ragged Schools	—	—	109	—
North-East London Mis. Halls (No. 1)	—	—	200	—
,, ,, (No. 2)	—	—	300	—
,, ,, (No. 3)	—	—	250	—
,, ,, (No. 5)	—	—	125	—
(*Mr. Chorley.*)				
Four Small Halls (*Mr. Chorley.*)	—	—	196	—

Missions.	Morning.	Afternoon.	Evening.	Accom.
Unitarian—				
Mission, 365, Cambridge-road	—	—	27	—
Evangelical Mission—				
Dalston Mission, 105, Dalston-lane	21	—	82	140
(*Mr. C. Russell Hurditch.*)				
Young Men's Christian Association—				
Y.M.C.A., 275, Mare-street, Hackney	—	60	200	350
(*Mr. F. L. Porter, Hon. Sec.*)				
Salvation Army—				
Hackney Salvation Army Barracks { 7 a.m. 11 / 11 a.m. 102 }		166	338	420
(*Capt. W. H. Nicholls.*)				
Stoke Newington { 7 a.m. 18 / 11 a.m. 154 }		168	361	350
(*Capt. Tutt.*)				

ST. GILES'.

Comprising the Sub-Districts of St. George, Bloomsbury; St. Giles, South; St. Giles, North.

	Morning.	Afternoon.	Evening.	Accom.
Church of England—				
St. George's Mission, Little Coram-st.	—	—	47	90
(*Rev. A. B. Carpenter.*)				
Sardinia-street Mission Church	—	—	43	—
(*Rev. David Rice-Jones.*)				
Short's Gardens Mission	40	—	110	—
(*Canon Nisbet.*)				
Baptist—				
Brook-st., St. Giles' Christian Mission	—	140	80	—
(*Mr. G. Hatton.*)				
Neal-street	46	—	142	500
(*Mr. G. Hatton.*)				
Wesleyan—				
St. Giles' Swiss Church, Endell-st.	—	—	40	200
(*Rev. Jakob Urech.*)				
Undenominational—				
St. Giles' Chn. Institute, High Holborn	—	150	50	360
(*Mr. E. Saunders.*)				
Coffee Palace, Newton-st., Holborn	—	—	29	—
(*Mr. W. List.*)				
Medical Mission—				
Medical Miss., Endell-st., Long Acre	—	—	95	130
(*Mr. F. A. Pring.*)				

STRAND.

COMPRISING THE SUB-DISTRICTS OF ST. MARTIN-IN-THE-FIELDS; ST. MARY-LE-STRAND; ST. CLEMENT DANES.

MISSIONS.	MORNING.	AFTERNOON.	EVENING.	ACCOM.
Church of England—				
Clare Market Mission (Rev. R. Thomas.)	—	—	83	—
Baptist—				
St. Giles' Ch. Mis., Wild-st., Drury-lane (Mr. G. Hatton.)	130	—	540	900
Brewer's-ct., St. Giles' Ch. Mis., „ „ (Mr. G. Hatton; Mr. G. Andrews.)	—	—	218	150
Undenominational—				
Betterton-street Mission, Drury-lane	—	—	62	150
Newchurch-court Mission	—	—	38	—
White Horse-yard Miss., Stanhope-st. (Mr. J. Macdonald.)	—	—	32	35
Theatrical Mission—				
Workman's Hall, Drury-lane (Mr. Hambleton.)	—	—	166	—
Young Men's Christian Association—				
Exeter Hall, Strand (Mr. E. J. Kennedy; Mr. A. Burson.)	—	180	1150	3000

HOLBORN.

COMPRISING THE SUB-DISTRICTS OF ST. GEORGE-THE-MARTYR; ST. ANDREW, EASTERN; SAFFRON HILL; ST. JAMES, CLERKENWELL; AMWELL, PENTONVILLE, GOSWELL STREET, OLD STREET, CITY ROAD, WHITECROSS STREET, FINSBURY.

Church of England—				
St. John the Evangelist School Mission (Rev. H. T. Concy.)	—	—	27	—
St. George-the-Mtyr. Miss., Ormond-yd. (Rev. D. Craven, Rector.)	—	—	63	120
St. Peter's Mission, Brook-street (Rev. E. Canney.)	—	—	70	—
St. Paul's Mission, 85, Goswell-road (Rev. A. S. Herring.)	—	80	{ 190 } { 55 }	—
Allen Street Mission, Goswell-rd. Hall	—	600	—	—
St. Stephen's Mis., 90, White Lion-st. (Rev. W. Leach.)	—	—	69	—
St. Clement's Mission, Lever-street (Rev. F. P. Downman.)	—	—	87	—

Missions.	Morning.	Afternoon.	Evening.	Accom.
Baptist—				
St. Giles' Christian Mission, Brook-st.	—	140	80	—
(Mr. G. Hatton.)				
Wesleyan—				
Radnor-street Mission.	—	—	138	180
(Mr. H. J. Cooper.)				
Castle-street Hall, Finsbury	—	100	60	100
Friends—				
Mis. Memorial Buildings, Roscoe-st.	507	115	284	490
(Mr. J. Allen Baker, Sec.)				
Meeting House, 32, St. John's-lane	23	61	42	350
(Mr. John D. Appleton.)				
Juv. Chris. Mis., Board Sch., Eagle-ct.	—	170	130	—
(Mr. T. Craft.)				
Unitarian—				
George-row Mission, St. Luke's	130	—	150	200
(Rev. F. Summers.)				
Christian Community—				
Mission, 135, Old-street, E.C.	—	—	80	150
(Mr. A. W. Sidey.)				
Young Men's Christian Association—				
Finsbury-park Hall, Seven Sisters' rd.	—	—	798	800
(Mr. R. A. Elvery.)				
Salvation Army—				
Salvation Army, Grecian Theatre	{ 7 a.m. 84 } { 11 a.m. 320 }	550	2500	2700
(Capt. T. Biggs.)				
London City Mission—				
Fox and Knot Mission, Charterhouse.	—	—	53	200
(Rev. J. R. Ken. Bell; Mr. A. Hart.)				
Lamb and Flag Miss., 10, Red Lion-st.	48	280	324	560
(Mr. J. G. Jeffs; Mr. Geo. Bray.)				
Orde Hall Mission, Gt. Ormond-street	—	—	210	—
(Mr. J. A. Arnold.)				
Undenominational—				
Mission, 346, Goswell-road.	—	—	—	70
(Mr. Lacey.)				
Hope Mission, Banner-street, E.C.	23	—	79	150
(Mr. Samuel Moore.)				
Sermon-lane Mission, Pentonville	75	—	203	400
(Mr. Fuller.)				
Field-lane Refuges, Clerkenwell.	{ 86 } { 334 }	64	102	600
(Mr. P. Platt.)				

Missions.	Morn-ing.	After-noon.	Even-ing.	Ac-com.
Undenominational (*continued*)				
Wilmington Mission, St. Helena-place (*Mr. T. Brannigan.*)	—	—	75	—
Vincent-street Ragged School Mission (*Mr. B. A. Oldfield, Sec.*)	—	74	33	—
Holborn Workhouse, Gray's-inn-road. (*Mr. E. M. Davies, L.C.M.*)	—	53	—	—
Fox-court Mission, Gray's-inn-road (*Mr. E. M. Davies, L.C.M.*)	—	—	32	—
Gee-street Mission, Goswell-road	—	—	70	—
Casual Wards, Vine-street. (*Board of Guardians.*)	50	—	—	—
Bowling Green-lane Mission (*Mr. W. Catlin.*)	—	—	94	—
British Workman Hall, Plummer's-pl. (*Mr. W. Wiggs.*)	15	97	82	—
Rossie House, 35, Lamb's Conduit-st. (*Mr. H. B. Waller.*)	—	33	—	—
Holborn Town Hall (*Mr. C. M. Sawell.*)	—	222	457	1000
Clerkenwell-close Mission. (*Mr. W. Groom.*)	156	—	32	200
Foresters' Hall (*Mr. J. A. Groom.*)	—	—	1450	1300
Albert Christian Institute, Jenkins-yd. (*Mr. Sparrow.*)	—	11	{ 40 } { 54 }	100
Working Lads' Club, Emerald-street. (*Miss Geraldine Batt.*)	—	—	40	—
Wilson-street Mission, Finsbury	—	—	11	—

CITY OF LONDON.

Comprising the Sub-Districts of St. Botolph, Cripplegate; St. Sepulchre; St. Bride; All Hallows, Barking; Broad Street.

Congregational—

Darby-street Mission, Royal Mint-st. . (*Rev. A. Sandison.*)	—	—	400	300

Baptist—

Great Arthur-st. Mis., Golden-lane (*Mr. Reuben May.*)	{ 10 a.m. 750 } { 11 a.m. 400 }	30	302	700

MISSION HALLS—SHOREDITCH.

Missions.	Morning.	Afternoon.	Evening.	Accom.
Undenominational—				
Mission, 24, Dean-street, Fetter-lane .	—	13	18	40
(*Mr. R. Hottin; Mr. J. Nicholls.*)				
Leysian Mission, 199, Whitecross-st. .	—	—	85	—
(*Mr. F. G. Morden.*)				
Hatfield-street Mission, Golden-lane .	—	—	{152 / 57}	—
(*Mr. G. A. Robbottom, Hon. Sec.*)				
Mission, Artillery-street, Bishopsgate .	115	50	40	100
(*Mrs. S. Finn.*)				

SHOREDITCH.

Comprising the Sub-Districts of Holywell, St. Leonard, Hoxton New Town, Hoxton Old Town, Haggerston.

	Morning.	Afternoon.	Evening.	Accom.
Church of England—				
St. John the Baptist Mission, 32, St. John's-road, Hoxton . . .	—	54	—	55
(*Mr. C. A. Jamack; Mr. S. Brick.*)				
Hoxton Academy Schools Mission .	—	—	75	100
(*Rev. T. Priestley; Mr. A. Millership.*)				
Congregational—				
Christian Institute, 19, Coronet-street	—	—	70	100
(*Mr. J. Burtt.*)				
Shoreditch Mission Hall, Basing-pl. .	—	—	104	—
(*Mr. Spong, L.C.M.*)				
Do. Adjacent Lodging-house	—	—	35	—
(*Mr. Spong, L.C.M.*)				
Baptist—				
Wellington-street Mission School .	—	40	125	—
(*Mr. G. Newland.*)				
Shap-street Mission, Kingsland .	83	221	154	100
(*Rev. W. Cuff.*)				
Hope-street Hall, Kingsland .	—	—	75	100
(*Rev. W. Cuff.*)				
Costers' Hall, 234, Hoxton-street, N. .	312	—	457	600
(*Mr. W. J. Orsman.*)				
Kingsland-road Mission Hall .	—	—	86	150
(*Rev. W. Cuff.*)				
Wesleyan—				
James-street Mission, Haggerston .	—	—	62	—
(*Mr. R. T. Wills.*)				

Missions.	Morning.	Afternoon.	Evening.	Accom.
Presbyterian—				
Harvey-street Mission, Hoxton (*Mr. C. D. Double.*)	341	641	398	800
Friends—				
Shoreditch Chr. Mis. Hall, Drysdale-st. (*Mrs. Richard Allen; Miss Marriage.*)	—	—	37	100
Young Men's Christian Association—				
Y.M.C.A., Kingsland-road (*Mr. East.*)	—	—	130	130
Salvation Army—				
Salv. Army Barracks, Haggerston (*Capt. W. H. Little.*)	7 a.m. 10 / 11 a.m. 40	100	190	—
London City Mission—				
Bateman's-row Mission, Shoreditch (*Mr. Walker.*)	—	—	96	100
Undenominational—				
Shoreditch Town Hall (*Mr. E. Eisenstadt.*)	—	950	—	1200
Hoxton Hall Blue Ribbon Mission (*Mr. J. T. Rae, Hon. Sec.*)	42	—	230	900
Vincent-street Mission Hall, Hoxton (*Mr. R. Stocks.*)	—	—	33	150

WHITECHAPEL.

Comprising the Sub-Districts of Spitalfields, Mile End New Town, Whitechapel Church, Goodman's Fields, Aldgate.

	Morning.	Afternoon.	Evening.	Accom.
Church of England—				
Charlotte-street Mission, Whitechapel (*Mr. C. Jones.*)	—	—	100	150
Congregational—				
Gospel Hall, Osborn-pl., Whitechapel (*Mr. J. Sharpless.*)	40	—	273	400
Raven-street (*Mr. W. B. Murray, L.C.M.*)	—	—	124	160
Wesleyan—				
Church-street Mission, Spitalfields (*Rev. P. Thompson.*)	152	—	173	1200
Unitarian—				
Buxton-st. Mis., Mile End New Town (*Rev. J. Farnsworth.*)	—	—	70	200

MISSION HALLS—BETHNAL GREEN.

Missions.	Morning.	Afternoon.	Evening.	Accom.
Christian Community—				
Thrawl-street, Brick-lane (*Mr. J. Atkinson.*)	7 a.m. 170 11 a.m. 95	30	175	150
Mildmay Mission—				
36, Wellclose-square, Mission (*Mr. Wilkinson.*)	—	—	52	150
Salvation Army—				
Salvation Army, Whitechapel, E. (*Capt. T. Robertson.*)	7 a.m. 11 11 a.m. 60	200	400	1250
London City Mission—				
Lodging-house Mission, 1, Osborn-pl. (*Mr. Silberschmidt.*)	—	200	—	—
Lodging-house Mission, 3, Osborn-pl. (*Mr. Silberschmidt.*)	—	130	—	—
Undenominational—				
Mission Pavilion Theatre (*Mr. H. Ehrlich, Manager.*)	—	—	2593	4000
Victoria Home, Commercial-street, E. (*Mr. A. Wilké.*)	—	30	120	300
George-yard Mission, High-street (*Mr. G. Holland.*)	83	—	471	450
Old Montague-street, Whitechapel	—	29	163	—
King Edward Schools, King Edward-st. (*Mr. C. Montague.*)	127	141	533	476
Railway Mission.	17	79	105	—

BETHNAL GREEN.

COMPRISING THE SUB-DISTRICTS OF HACKNEY-ROAD; GREEN, BETHNAL-GREEN; CHURCH, BETHNAL-GREEN; TOWN, BETHNAL-GREEN.

Missions.	Morning.	Afternoon.	Evening.	Accom.
Church of England—				
78, Cranbrook-street (*Rev. G. Moon; Mr. H. W. Cook, L.C.M.*)	—	—	35	60
St. Philips' School Mission (*Mr. E. Webb, L.C.M.*)	—	—	25	100
Congregational—				
Old Nichol-street Mission (*Mr. R. Allinson.*)	30	—	91	300

Missions.	Morning.	Afternoon.	Evening.	Accom.
Baptist—				
Marnham Hall, Darling-row (*Mr. H. C. Willings.*)	—	—	70	200
Gibraltar Mission (*Rev. W. Cuff; Mr. W. G. Hayes.*)	—	247	274	400
Good Shepherd Mis., Three-Colt-lane (*Mr. Freer.*)	—	—	—	200
Mission, Old Bethnal Green-road	—	—	60	200
Wesleyan—				
Green-street Mission (*Mr. Jas. Jeremy.*)	—	—	36	100
Thomas'-passage, Brady-street (*Mr. W. Green, L.C.M.*)	41	100	43	200
Children's Home, Hartley-street (*Mr. F. Hills.*)	—	—	372	400
Tent-street Mission (*Mr. Renney.*)	—	—	70	150
Mildmay Mission—				
Mission Hall, Turville-square (*Miss L. Boura.*)	—	—	151	160
Mildmay Mission Hall, 12, Church-st (*Miss L. Bowie.*)	—	—	126	160
Brethren—				
Mission, 38, Alma-road	—	—	16	—
Open Brethren—				
Victoria Park-square Chapel (*Mr. W. Parr.*)	56	—	270	500
Christian Community—				
Memorial Hall, London-square (*Mr. G. F. Hilcken.*)	—	—	174	350
Salvation Army—				
Salvation Army Barracks (*Lieut. Burnell.*)	7 a.m. 9 / 10.30 a.m. 33	98	205	300
London City Mission—				
Parliament-street Mission Room (*Mr. Bartlett, Sec.; Mr. Barnes, Miss.*)	—	—	27	—
Brady-street Mission (*Mr. F. Passmore.*)	—	—	30	100
Shaftesbury Hall, Gosset-street (*Mr. E. King.*)	—	—	105	120

MISSION HALLS—ST. GEORGE-IN-THE-EAST.

Missions.	Morn-ing.	After-noon.	Even-ing.	Ac-com.
Undenominational—				
Green-street Mission Hall	12	25	64	200
Ashley Mission, Peel-grove	—	—	210	500
(*Miss Bontein.*)				
Old Zion Chapel Mission	—	—	56	—
(*Mr. H. Lockyer, L.C.M.*)				
Hope Town Hall, 203½, Bethnal-gr.-rd.	—	—	120	—
(*Mr. J. C. Hill, Sec.*)				
Lond. Open Air Temperance Mission	50	—	250	—
(*Mr. John Russell.*)				
Bethnal-green Mission	—	—	70	200
(*Mr. J. W. Maxwell, Sec.*)				

ST. GEORGE-IN-THE-EAST.

COMPRISING THE SUB-DISTRICTS OF ST. GEORGE (NORTH), AND ST. JOHN.

Church of England—				
St. George's-in-the-East Mission Hall	—	—	50	400
(*Mr. A. McGovern, Miss.; Rev. C. H. Turner, Rec.*)				
St. Geo.'s Mis., 137, St. George-street	110	—	50	150
(*Mr. R. Petherbridge.*)				
Christ Church Mission, Watney-street	—	—	103	150
(*Rev. W. P. Jay.*)				
Congregational—				
Mission Hall, Old Gravel-lane	—	—	82	300
(*Mr. E. Allen.*)				
Lucas-st. Mission, Commercial-road	—	—	24	—
(*Mr. Yeadell.*)				
Mission Hall, Anchor and Hope-alley	—	—	18	110
(*Mr. Roby.*)				
Ebenezer Hall, Watney-passage	—	—	{ 150 / 50 }	350
(*Miss E. Bowrey.*)				
Germans—				
Reading Room, Seaman's So., St. Geo.	—	10	—	—
(*Mr. Bottjer.*)				
Mission, 2, Plough-buildings { Wednesday, German Mis., 18 / Friday, Jews' Mission 26 / Saturday, Jews' Mission 34 }				—
(*Mr. Silberschmidt.*)				
London City Mission—				
Mission, Christian-street	—	—	38	70
(*Mr. A. Spong.*)				
Undenominational—				
Iron Hall, Wapping	—	—	75	—
(*Mr. F. N. Charrington.*)				

6

Missions.	Morning.	Afternoon.	Evening.	Accom.
Undenominational *(continued)*—				
Seaman's Chapel, St. George-street	85	—	169	250
(*Rev. G. J. Hill.*)				
Seaman's Bethel, Old Gravel-lane	54	—	51	220
(*Rev. T. R. Couch.*)				
Sailors' Home, Dock-st., London Dock	9	—	12	90
(*Mr. W. R. Carroll.*)				

STEPNEY.

Comprising the Sub-Districts of Shadwell, Ratcliff, and Limehouse.

Missions.	Morning.	Afternoon.	Evening.	Accom.
Church of England—				
Heath-street Mis., Commercial-road	—	—	52	50
(*Rev. E. C. Evans.*)				
Grosvenor-street Mission, Stepney	—	—	67	160
(*Rev. E. C. Evans.*)				
St. Matthias' Mission, Railway-arch	—	—	115	300
(*Rev. W. Gray.*)				
Cologne-street, Whitechapel	—	—	33	120
Baptist—				
Mission Chapel, Devonport-street	—	—	104	275
(*Mr. S. J. Lancaster.*)				
Salvation Army—				
Salvation Army, Limehouse	7 a.m. 5 / 11 a.m. 100	180	300	450
(*Capt. J. Robertson.*)				
London City Mission—				
Love-lane Mission	—	—	291	350
(*Mr. G. Harris.*)				
Twine-court, Cable-street, Shadwell	—	—	60	100
(*Mr. R. Yeeles.*)				
Silver-street, Stepney-green	—	—	30	80
(*Mr. W. A. Wittey.*)				
Undenominational—				
Sailor's Institute, Shadwell	no return	Sailors	—	650
(*Rev. E. W. Matthews.*)				
Devonport-street Gospel Mission	12	—	16	170
(*Mr. E. C. Smith.*)				
Edinburgh Castle, Rhodeswell-road	1291 / 536	875	1946	3500
(*Dr. Barnardo.*)				
Dorcas Home Mission, Carr-street	—	—	123	500
(*Dr. Barnardo.*)				
Medical Mission, High-st., Shadwell	—	—	72	150
(*Dr. Barnardo.*)				

MILE END OLD TOWN.

COMPRISING THE SUB-DISTRICTS OF MILE END OLD TOWN (WESTERN), AND MILE END OLD TOWN (EASTERN).

Missions.	Morn- ing.	After- noon.	Even- ing.	Ac- com.
Church of England—				
St. Benet's Hall, Mile End-road .	—	—	222	200
(*Rev. Thomas Richardson.*)				
Skinner's Chapel, Mile End-road	—	9	—	20
(*Rev. F. H. Dinnis.*)				
St. Thomas' Mission, Bromehead-st. .	—	—	31	70
(*Rev. A. W. Cribb.*)				
Congregational—				
Ernest-street Mission .	—	—	48	120
(*Mr. McArthur.*)				
Wesleyan—				
Gordon Hall, Globe-road	160	—	486	500
(*Dr. Stephenson.*)				
Presbyterian—				
Silvertown Mission	100	—	180	—
(*Rev. Francis Slade.*)				
Salvation Army—				
Salvation Army, Silvertown	{ 7 a.m. 22 11 a.m. 35 }	65	110	120
(*Capt. E. Palmer.*)				
Undenominational—				
Gt. Assembly Hall, Mile End-road	1195	—	3759	4500
(*Mr. F. N. Charrington.*)				
Mission, 332, Mile End-road	90	—	75	—
Leopold House, Burdett-road, E.	—	—	209	300
(*Mr. R. Fell.*)				
Ben Jonson-road Hall	—	—	51	—
Free Gospel Mission, 59, Mile End-rd.	40	140	220	260
(*Mr. G. Hamilton.*)				

POPLAR.

COMPRISING THE SUB-DISTRICTS OF BOW, BROMLEY, AND POPLAR.

Church of England—				
Bromley Mission	161	—	116	200
(*Rev. Mr. Poole.*)				
St. Mark's Mission Hall, Victoria-park	87	369	—	400
(*Rev. Matthew Sweetman, Vicar.*)				
Park-hall, Dace-road .	—	—	85	250

Missions.	Morning.	Afternoon.	Evening.	Accom.
Church of England (*continued*)—				
Christ Church Mission, Old Ford-road	97	150	63	300
(*Rev. H. A. S. Pitt.*)				
Reading Room, St. Stephen's	—	40	—	—
(*Rev. J. P. Thompson.*)				
St. Stephen's Mission, Bow	—	—	57	150
(*Rev. R. Elliott, Curate.*)				
Congregational—				
North Bow Mission Hall, Armagh-st.	—	—	157	250
(*Mr. Maccullam.*)				
Bow and Bromley Institute	—	—	668	1200
(*Rev. W. E. Hurndall.*)				
Shaftesbury Hall, Arnold-road, Bow	—	—	116	150
(*Mr. Hellyer.*)				
Baptist—				
Bow Coffee Palace, Bow-road	—	—	60	200
(*Mr. W. Hayward, Harley House.*)				
Berger Hall, Epsom-street	60	—	230	900
(*Mr. W. Hayward.*)				
Harley Hall, Devons-road, Bow	—	—	100	300
(*Mr. W. Hayward.*)				
Tryphena Gospel, Bow Common-lane	—	—	—	200
(*Rev. A. Brown; Mr. B. J. Adams.*)				
Wesleyan—				
Albert-terrace, Bow	—	—	25	200
(*Rev. E. Banham.*)				
Swanscombe-st., Barking-rd. (German)	20	—	27	100
(*Rev. J. Urech.*)				
Primitive Methodist—				
Powis-road Mission, Bromley-by-Bow	30	—	60	400
(*Mr. W. Bould.*)				
Christian Community—				
115, Poplar High-street	36	—	84	150
(*Mr. J. Knibbs.*)				
London City Mission—				
Hall, 77, Augusta-street, Poplar	—	—	45	100
(*Mr. J. Aulds.*)				
East-street Mission Hall, Stratford	—	—	30	50
(*Mr. Allman.*)				
Grundy-street Mission Hall, Stratford	—	—	130	100
(*Mr. O. Siden.*)				
City Mission-station, Francis-street	—	33	58	80
(*Mr. W. Tarr.*)				
People's Hall, Bow Common-lane	75	—	138	300

MISSION HALLS—POPLAR.

Missions.	Morn- ing.	After- noon.	Even- ing.	Ac- com.
London City Mission *(continued)*—				
Memorial Hall, 118, Balaam-street (*Mr. W. Hudson.*)	—	28	26	80
Shipwright's-ter., Brunswick-street (*Mr. Thomas Harwood.*)	—	—	53	80
Railway Mission, 103, Fairfield-road (*Mr. W. Vicary.*)	—	57	55	200
Stebondale-street, Cubitt-town (*Mr. Morrish.*)	—	—	80	150
Francis-street, Stratford (*Mr. Gage.*)	—	—	122	130
Undenominational—				
Millwall Juvenile, 1, Tobago-street	—	—	115	117
Railway Mis., Leyton House, Stratford (*Miss Davidson.*)	—	224	—	196
Old Ford Mis., Tredegar road, Bow (*Mr. A. Farnan*)	—	—	78	400
Brunswick Hall, Brunswick-road	—	—	250	250
Ashburton House, Custom House-ter. (*Lady Ashburton; Mr. N. R. Hughman.*)	96	—	148	150
Axe-street Meeting, Barking (*Mr. A. Bowles; Mr. W. T. Float.*)	—	—	185	200
Evangelical Mission—				
Bignold Hall, Bignold-road (*Mr. C. Russell Hurditch.*)	112	65	360	—
Salvation Army—				
Salvation Army, Canning-town (*Capt. A. Saker Lynne.*)	{ 7 a.m. 19 { 11 a.m. 45	132	172	150
Salvation Army, Leyton (*Capt. A. Harrison.*)	{ 7 a.m. 41 { 11 a.m. 130	259	392	450
Salvation Army, Poplar (*Capt. A. Camp.*)	{ 7 a.m. 12 { 11 a.m. 70	220	300	400
Salvation Army, Plaistow (*Capt. E. E. Lock.*)	{ 7 a.m. 8 { 11 a.m. 58	146	196	200
Salvation Army, Stratford (*Capt. L. Barritt.*)	{ 7 a.m. 16 { 11 a.m. 150	250	520	1800

ST. SAVIOUR, SOUTHWARK.

Comprising the Sub-districts of Christ Church, Southwark; St. Saviour; Kent-road; Borough-road; London-road; Trinity, Newington; St. Peter, Walworth; St. Mary, Newington.

Missions.	Morning.	Afternoon.	Evening.	Accom.
Church of England—				
St. Matthew Mis. Room, New Kent-rd.	14	—	36	250
(Rev. W. J. A. Sturdee.)				
Congregational—				
Culmore-road Hall, Old Kent-road	47	—	182	—
Farm House Mission, Harrow-street	50	—	182	100
(Mr. S. Hunter, Hon. Sec.)				
Mission, Collier's Rents, Bermondsey	—	—	59	450
(Mr. Smith.)				
Baptist—				
Victory-place Institute, Walworth	—	—	20	250
(Mr. F. Brumwell; Mr. Whiterick.)				
Workman's Mission, 4, York-street	—	—	80	200
(Mr. H. Young.)				
Y.M.C.A. Inst., Newington-Causeway	—	—	101	200
(Mr. H. Elvin; Mr. H. R. Hammond.)				
Mission Hall, 1, Harrow-st., Lant-st.	—	—	68	150
(Mr. G. Jeffery.)				
People's Gospel Hall, Townsend-st.	—	—	78	150
(Mr. G. Gregory.)				
Almshouses Mission, Walworth-road	—	—	113	—
(Mr. G. A. Maples.)				
Maze Pond Miss., 18, St. Thomas-rd	—	—	46	54
(Mr. F. E. Bursell, Hon. Sec.)				
Miss. Hall, Boddy's Bridge, Ground-st.	25	58	48	—
(Rev. C. H. Spurgeon.)				
Surrey-square Mission, Old Kent-road	128	—	178	—
(Rev. C. H. Spurgeon.)				
Methodist New Connexion—				
Mission, 162, Walworth-road, S.E.	40	—	60	—
(Rev. W. W. Howard.)				
Mildmay Mission—				
Mission, 6A, Trinity-st., Blackman-st.	—	—	65	—
(Mr. J. E. Mathieson.)				
St. Peter's Mission, 5 Bronte-place	—	—	69	—
(Mr. L. S. Ling.)				
Christian Community—				
Shaftesbury Hall, 179, Tabard-street	—	—	24	—
(Mr. G. H. Breton.)				

MISSION HALLS—ST. OLAVE, SOUTHWARK.

Missions.	Morning.	Afternoon.	Evening.	Accom.
London City Mission—				
Mission, Pepper-st., Union-st., Boro'. (*Mr. Belcham.*)	—	—	58	100
Cole-st. Hall, Great Dover-street (*Mr. Pike.*)	—	—	51	250
Mission Room, 56, Friar-street (*Mr. T. Edwards.*)	—	—	50	100
Camden Chislehurst Mission, Earl-st. (*Mr. C. Hill.*)	—	—	85	—
School Missn., York-st., Walworth-rd. (*Mr. Bachell.*)	—	17	—	50
Townley-st. Mission, New Kent-road (*Mr. Tomkins.*)	—	—	40	65
New-st. Mission, Borough-road (*Mr. S. Sewell.*)	—	—	45	160
Deacon-st. Missn. Hall, Walworth-rd. (*Mr. Kelly.*)	—	—	30	50
Mission Hall, Webber-st. Blackfriars (*Mr. N. S. Licence.*)	—	—	33	60
Boro' Market Mission Hall, Borough (*Mr. James Morris.*)	40	—	62	—
Salvation Army—				
Salvation Army, Borough Corps (*Capt. J. Sawyer.*)	{ 7 a.m. 34 } { 11 a.m. 180 }	400	760	800
Salvtn. Army Hall, 34, Westcott-st. (*Capt. Mrs. Webb.*)	11	29	113	200
Undenominational—				
King's Court Hall, Great Suffolk-st. (*Mr. T. Hunter; Mr. J. Benford, Sec.*)	40	150	70	200
Arthur-street Mission, Old Kent-rd.		No service.		

ST. OLAVE, SOUTHWARK.

Comprising the Sub-Districts of St. Olave; Leather Market; St. Mary Magdalen; St. James, Bermondsey; Rotherhithe.

Missions.	Morning.	Afternoon.	Evening.	Accom.
Church of England—				
St. Crispin's Mis., Cherry Garden-st. (*Rev. W. Powell.*)	—	—	21	—
St. Luke, 20A, Alfred-st., Bermondsey (*Mr. Pridmore.*)	—	—	56	160
St. James's Mission, St. James's-road (*Rev. J. S. Brownhill, Curate.*)	—	40	50	300

MISSIONS.	MORN-ING.	AFTER-NOON.	EVEN-ING.	AC-COM.
Church of England (*continued*)—				
Clare College Mission, Abbeyfield-rd.	238	380	234	200
(*Rev. E. King.*)				
St. Katherine's, St. Helena's-gardens .	495	—	—	300
(*Rev. T. C. Johnson.*)				
Congregational—				
Salisbury-st. Hall, Bermondsey .	—	—	28	150
(*Rev. J. Farrar.*)				
Mission Hall, Gedling-street	—	—	61	—
Baptist—				
Haddon Hall, Bermondsey New-road	161	—	444	600
(*Mr. Olney, jun.*)				
Long-lane Mission	—	—	170	150
(*Mr. W. Baker, L.C.M.*)				
Verney-road, late Milledge-st., Mission	—	—	145	230
(*Rev. B. Brigg ; Mr. Charles Grose.*)				
Mission Hall, Little George-street	30	114	80	—
(*Rev. C. H. Spurgeon.*)				
Wesleyan—				
Silver-street Mission, Rotherhithe	89	—	78	450
London City Mission—				
Gedling-street Schools	—	—	187	400
(*Mr. Davis ; Mr. Osborne.*)	—	—	97	—
Mission Hall, 23, Hickman's Folly	—	—	54	100
(*Mr. O. S. Gray.*)				
Abbey-street Mission, Bermondsey .	—	—	130	300
(*Mr. T. W. New.*)				
Tabard Mission Hall, 210, Weston-st.	16	—	55	—
(*Mr. R. A. Hulls.*)				
Mission Hall, 209, Weston-street	—	—	58	70
(*Mr. W. Narroway.*)				
Alexandra Temp. Hall, Sthwrk.-pk.-rd.	—	—	145	200
(*Mr. J. Whitburn.*)				
Mission Hall, Cornbury-road	—	40	50	80
(*Mr. T. Sunshine.*)				
Abbey-street Schools Mission	—	—	46	250
(*Mr. E. T. Kennett.*)				
Mildmay Mission—				
St. James's Hall, New Church-street .	—	75	90	—
(*Mrs. Pennefather.*)				
Salvation Army—				
Rotherhithe Corps .	{ 7 a.m. 50 } { 10.30 a.m. 200 }	500	1200	1460
(*Capt. Howe.*)				

MISSION HALLS—LAMBETH.

MISSIONS.	MORN-ING.	AFTER-NOON.	EVEN-ING.	AC-COM.
Young Men's Christian Association—				
Mission Hall, Melior-st., Bermondsey	50	—	160	180
Mr. N. R. Hughman, Hon. Sec.	30			
Undenominational—				
Memorial Hall, Paradise-street	29	9	167	250
(*Miss Barclay.*)				
The Ark Mission, Paradise-street	41	—	50	300
Anchor Missn., Butler's-pl., Dockhead	—	—	87	250
(*Mr. Wontner.*)				
Seaman's Mission Hall, Derrick-street	98	—	62	150
London-street Mission, Dockhead	—	—	92	150
" " " "	—	—	86	—
(*Mr. W. Rycell.*)				
Gospel Mission, Oldfield-road	78	92	68	85
(*Mr. L. E. Atkins.*)				

LAMBETH.

COMPRISING THE SUB-DISTRICTS OF WATERLOO-ROAD 1ST, WATERLOO-ROAD 2ND, LAMBETH CHURCH 1ST, LAMBETH CHURCH 2ND, KENNINGTON 1ST, KENNINGTON 2ND, BRIXTON, AND NORWOOD.

Church of England—

St. Stephen's, John-street, Dorset-road	—	—	45	50
(*Rev. J. Stephen.*)				
Roupel-st. Mis., St. Andrew's Schools	—	—	98	450
(*Rev. Trevor Fielder.*)				
St. Paul's Beehive Mission, Brixton	10	—	50	—
(*Rev. G. B. Concanon.*)				
St. Mark's Mission, Kennington	267	—	121	—
(*Rev. H. H. Montgomery.*)				
St. Mark's Mission, Bolton-street	220	—	112	400
(*Rev. H. H. Montgomery.*)				
St. Mark's Mission, Church-st. School	70	—	—	—
(*Rev. H. H. Montgomery.*)				
St. Mary's Mission, 25, Lambeth-walk	—	—	71	—
(*Hon. and Rev. Canon Pelham.*)				
Christ Church Mission, North Brixton	—	—	72	500
(*Mr. A. Ricarby, Hon. Sec.*)				
St. Luke's Mission, West Norwood	—	—	41	—
(*Rev. J. Gilmore.*)				
St. Mary-the-Less Mission, Kennington	—	—	54	600
(*Rev. G. H. Bromfield.*)				
St. Thomas' Schools, Waterloo-road	—	—	160	450
(*Rev. C. F. Seymour.*)				

Missions.	Morn-ing.	After-noon.	Even-ing.	Accom·
Church of England (*continued*)—				
Emmanuel Ch. Mis., West Dulwich	—	—	33	200
(*Rev. E. Rae, Vicar.*)				
Star Mission, Lambeth-walk	—	—	59	70
(*Rev. Canon Pelham.*)				
St. Andrew's Mission, Landor-road	18	—	100	—
(*Rev. C. E. Escreet.*)				
St. Jude's Mission, Herne-hill	105	—	52	400
(*Rev. R. B. Ransford.*)				
Victoria Hall, Waterloo-road	—	—	408	—
(*Mr. N. F. Horne, Hon. Sec.*)				
Church Army—				
Stockwell Church Army	—	—	190	500
(*Capt. E. Porter.*)				
Congregational—				
Christ Church, Westminster-road	—	326	—	800
(*Rev. Newman Hall.*)				
Lower Hawkstone Hall	—	—	61	120
(*Mr. W. Benson.*)				
Mission Hall, Russell-street, Brixton	—	—	73	400
(*Rev. Dr. Stevenson.*)				
Lambeth Baths Gospel Temp. Mis.	220	—	342	2000
(*Rev. W. Mottram.*)				
Rowland Hill Schoolroom	—	—	22	50
(*Mr. Legg, L.C.M.*)				
Baptist—				
Mission Chapel, Cornwall-rd., Brixton	94	—	90	500
(*Mr. R. J. Greenwood.*)				
Brixton Tabernacle, Stockwell-road	182	—	169	—
(*Rev. C. Cornwell.*)				
Albert Hall, Albert Embankment	—	—	36	—
Working Men's Hall, Collingwood-st.	—	—	500	600
(*Messrs. S. and J. Young.*)				
Oakley-street Mission	—	—	80	85
(*Mr. J. Lovejoy.*)				
Spiller's-court, Webber-row	—	—	52	50
(*Mr. W. E. Everett.*)				
Wesleyan—				
New-street Mission, Lambeth-walk	—	—	55	200
Mission Hall, Lyham-road, Brixton	87	—	302	300
(*Mr. T. J. Gardiner.*)				
Mission Hall, 89, Dulwich-road	58	147	195	250
(*Mr. F. Agnew, Hon. Sec.*)				
Young Men's Christian Association—				
Brixton Hall	—	—	550	700
(*Mr. G. E. Williams.*)				

MISSION HALLS—LAMBETH.

Missions.	Morning.	Afternoon.	Evening.	Accom.
Salvation Army—				
Blackfriars Corps, No. 1056 (*Capt. Alice Lewis.*)	7 a.m. 21 11 a.m. 90	400	470	450
Upper Norwood Barracks (*Capt. P. Ashton.*)	7 a.m. 36 11 a.m. 202	384	728	800
Brixton Corps (*Capt. Jackson.*)	7 a.m. 29 10.30 a.m. 109	198	220	200
London City Mission—				
Park-road, Brixton-hill (*Mr. W. Baker.*)	—	—	170	150
Mission Hall, Blind-corner, Norwood (*Mr. Frank King.*)	—	51	121	120
Windmill-st. Mission Hall, New Cut (*Mr. W. T. Delves.*)	—	—	31	50
Mason-st. Mis. Room, Westmr.-br.-rd. (*Mr. B. T. Case.*)	—	—	40	40
Cottage-pl. Mission, Commercial-rd. (*Mr. C. Wheeler.*)	—	—	68	—
Anne-street Hall, Waterloo-road (*Mr. W. Goodall.*)	—	—	45	65
Mission Room, Romany-rd., Norwood (*Mr. H. Baston.*)	—	51	—	70
City Mission Room, 39, Gloucester-st. (*Mr. M. Dunkley.*)	—	—	49	60
North-street Hall, Kennington-road (*Mr. W. H. Joy.*)	—	—	41	200
George-street Schools (*Mr. G. Goodman.*)	—	—	110	—
Moffat Institute, 92, Vauxhall-street (*Mr. T. Walmsley.*)	—	—	96	150
Mission, 197, Lyham-road (*Mr. W. Coles.*)	—	26	85	—
North-street Mission Hall, Kennington (*Rev. H. Grainger.*)	—	—	41	—
Railway Mission, Loughboro' Station (*Mr. C. Goddard.*)	—	—	130	200
Granby-place Mission, Lower Marsh (*Mr. W. Passingham.*)	—	—	36	70
Undenominational—				
Victoria Hall, Waterloo-road (*Miss Kate Rivary.*)	—	90	—	—
New Hall-street, West Norwood	29	49	36	200
Brixton Christian Mission, Sussex-rd.	62	—	81	106

Missions.	Morn- ing.	After- noon.	Even- ing.	Ac- com.
Undenominational (*continued*)—				
St. James' Temperance Mission Hall	43	—	139	1200
(*Mr. C. Zierenburg.*)				
Auckland Hall, West Norwood	—	—	136	300
(*Mr. T. W. Stoughton.*)				
Clive Hall, Clive-road, West Norwood	55	—	52	—
Conference Hall, Norwood-road	31	30	151	—
(*Miss A. Sawede.*)				
Grosmont Endlesham-road, Balham	87	—	152	—
(*Mr. E. Powell.*)				
Blackfriars Mission, 33, New Cut	73	—	44	—
Gospel Hall, 15, New Cut	58	177	95	—
Leafield Hall, Norwood	—	20	—	—
Mission, Cornwall-road, Stamford-st.	—	—	19	80
Gospel Hall, Railton-road, Brixton	60	104	60	—
Rosemary Hall, Brixton	133	—	137	—

WANDSWORTH.

COMPRISING THE SUB-DISTRICTS OF CLAPHAM, EAST BATTERSEA, WEST BATTERSEA, WANDSWORTH, PUTNEY, AND STREATHAM.

Missions.	Morn- ing.	After- noon.	Even- ing.	Ac- com.
Church of England—				
St. James', Ponton road, Nine Elms	120	—	80	200
(*Rev. C. Rhodes Hall.*)				
St. Paul's Mission Hall, Heath-road	—	—	51	300
St. Andrews' Mission, Garratt-lane	—	—	151	—
(*Rev. T. S. Colman.*)				
Immanuel Church Mission, Eardley-rd.	—	—	122	—
(*Rev. F. E. Browett, Curate.*)				
St. Stephen's Mission, Point Pleasant	—	—	100	200
(*Rev. C. Carruthers, Vicar.*)				
St. James' Mission, Nine Elms-lane	93	—	86	200
(*Rev. C. Rhodes Hall.*)				
St. George's Mis., New-rd., Battersea	—	—	50	250
(*Mr. Vellenowith.*)				
St. Ann's, Garratt-lane, Tooting	—	—	15	—
(*Rev. T. S. Colman.*)				
Point Mission Room, Wandsworth	—	—	130	250
Belmore-street Mission	—	—	37	—
Church Army—				
Church Army, Battersea	—	—	120	—
(*Capt. Howes; Rev. J. Holyroyd.*)				
Congregational—				
Milton Hall Mission	72	—	164	350
(*Rev. W. Daniel.*)				
Ceylon-street, Battersea Park-road	—	—	38	70
(*Mr. P. A. Neville, L.C.M.*)				

MISSION HALLS—WANDSWORTH.

Missions.	Morn-ing.	After-noon.	Even-ing.	Ac-com.
Congregational *continued*)—				
Dunt's-hill, Earlsfield-road	68	—	240	350
(*Mr. C. Mathieson Smith.*)				
Memorial Hall, High-street	—	—	100	400
(*Mr. J. Simms, L.C.M.*)				
Mission Hall, Queen's-place	—	—	105	200
(*Mr. A. Gleff, Hon. Sec.*)				
Union Ch. Mis., Cooper's Arms-lane	—	—	59	75
(*Mr. A. Mayers, Hon. Sec.*)				
Zennor-road Mission, Balham	—	26	100	100
Baptist—				
British School, Plough-lane	—	—	25	100
(*Mr. R. H. Miles, L.C.M.*)				
Lonesome Mission Hall	29	—	60	90
(*Mr. A. J. Broad, Sec.*)				
Onward Christian Room, York-road	—	—	33	70
(*Mr. Gauntlett.*)				
Park Town Hall, Queen's-road	—	—	70	200
(*Rev. C. H. Spurgeon.*)				
Renshaw-street	—	19	68	64
(*Mr. J. Gleazer.*)				
Presbyterian—				
Trinity Hall, Stewart's-road	115	—	218	400
(*Mr. R. Noble.*)				
Mission, 16, Wellford-road, Streatham	—	—	63	—
(*Mr. John G. Smieton.*)				
Spread Eagle Rooms, Wandsworth	—	—	205	400
(*Misses Bell, Berry, Boyd, and Cunningham.*)				
Wesleyan—				
Waterside Mission	240	308	176	220
(*Mr. D. F. Shillington.*)				
Mission, Garrett-lane, Wandsworth	—	—	105	—
Immanuel Mission Hall, Selkirk-road	—	—	116	150
Culvert-road, Battersea Park-road	29	—	272	300
(*Mr. C. J. Blatchley.*)				
West Streatham Mission	—	—	80	80
(*Rev. F. J. Sharr.*)				
Swaby-road, Broomwood-park	61	—	55	120
(*Rev. R. Culley.*)				
Surrey-lane, Battersea	—	—	38	40
(*Mr. C. J. Blatchley*)				
Primitive Methodist—				
Balham New-road Mission	71	—	61	—
Evangelistic Mission—				
Rest Mission Room, Mortlake	—	85	97	150
(*Mr. C. R. Hurditch.*)				

THE RELIGIOUS CENSUS OF LONDON.

MISSIONS.	MORNING.	AFTERNOON.	EVENING.	ACCOM.
Salvation Army—				
Sal. Army Bks., 43, Lockington-rd. (*Capt. B. Stone.*)	7 a.m. 26 11 a.m. 200	350	800	700
Sal. Army Bks., High-st. Battersea (*Capt. J. T. Morris.*)	7 p.m. 30 11 a.m. 150	450	835	900
Sal. Army Bks., Winstanley-rd. (*Capt. Arnott.*)	7 a.m. 1 11 a.m. 20	40	70	120
Salvation Army (*Capt. Giles.*)	7 a.m. 8 11 a.m. 150	280	450	400
London City Mission—				
Mission Hall, South-street (*Mr. J. Dawson.*)	—	—	50	—
Mission, St. Culvert-road (*Mr. Smith.*)	—	—	40	80
High-street Mission, Clapham (*Mr. McNally.*)	—	—	55	—
Mission, Bath Room, York-road (*Mr. J. Warren.*)	—	87	110	200
Tyneham Hall, Clapham (*Rev. E. Greville.*)	—	—	140	260
Mission Room, Lilleshall-road (*Mr. T. J. Jackson.*)	—	23	50	100
White-square Mission, Clapham (*Mr. A. J. Leighton.*)	—	10	190	150
Star and Anchor Hall, King's-road	—	—	54	70
Mission, 10, Ceylon-street, Battersea (*Mr. P. A. Neville.*)	—	11	21	60
Undenominational—				
High-street, Battersea	—	—	150	—
Shaftesbury Hall, Ashbury-road (*Mr. E. Collier.*)	—	—	140	270
Howard-street Mission, New-road (*Mr. J. Soames.*)	130	143	105	150
Mission, 90, High street, Putney	32	—	42	—
Down Lodge Hall, High-street (*Mr. C. F. Davis, Hon. Sec.*)	—	118	467	573
Farm Stables Mission, Clapham-road (*Miss Clara Harris.*)	—	—	33	—
Conference Hall, Clapham-road	—	—	100	—
Mill Pond Bridge Mission, Nine Elms	—	—	93	—
Railway Mission, 443, Wandsworth-rd.	—	23	52	—
Mission Hall, Merton-road (*Mr. J. Evans.*)	—	57	94	130

Missions.	Morn-ing.	After-noon.	Even-ing.	Ac-com.
Undenominational (*continued*)—				
Mission, High-street, Battersea	125	300	150	—
Platt Mission, Putney	30	60	150	—
Speke Hall, Speke-road	110	—	397	—

CAMBERWELL.
Comprising the Sub-Districts of Dulwich, Camberwell, Peckham, and St. George.

Missions.	Morn-ing.	After-noon.	Even-ing.	Ac-com.
Church of England—				
Trinity College Mis., 265, Albany-road (*Rev. Byrom Holland.*)	—	—	93	150
Foxbury-road Mission, Hatcham (*Capt. Francis, C.A.*)	90	100	146	300
Woodpecker-road Mission, Hatcham (*Capt. Francis, C.A.*)	—	—	45	50
St. Bartholomew (*Rev. Henry Wells.*)	608	—	740	—
Congregational—				
Goldie-street, Coburg-road (*Mr. W. Pim, L.C.M.*)	—	—	50	100
Mission Chapel, Besson-street (*Rev. G. B. Ryley.*)	85	—	105	180
Linnell-road Mission (*Mr. R. A. Wickson, Sec.*)	—	—	35	42
Clifton Cong. Church Mission Hall (*Mr. A. J. Matthews.*)	—	—	60	100
Working Men's Inst., Waterloo-street (*Mr. J. Matthews, Miss.*)	—	25	200	420
Ledbury-street Mission, Peckham (*Mr. J. W. Polkinghorne.*)	46	—	25	110
Ragged School Mission, Toulon-street (*Rev. D. A. Herschell.*)	—	—	120	450
Mis. Hall, corner of Lorrimore-road (*Rev. J. P. Gent.*)	—	—	52	—
Lothian-road Chapel Mission (*Rev. J. P. Gent.*)	—	—	30	—
Baptist—				
Gospel Hall, Blenheim-grove (*Mr. H. Camp.*)	40	—	35	200
Crawford-street Mission (*Mr. J. Wilson.*)	—	—	80	—
Mansion House-square Mission (*Mr. G. W. Linnecar.*)	139	—	322	600
Gunton-place, Peckham Rye (*Mr. Cambrell.*)	25	—	85	85
Sumner-road Mission, Peckham (*Mr. Scarr.*)	—	—	63	100

Missions.	Morn-ing.	After-noon.	Even-ing.	Ac-com.
Baptist (*continued*)—				
George-street Mission Hall (*Mr. Dale.*)	38	—	101	150
Goldsmith-road Mission (*Mr. J. Hodson, Sec.*)	—	—	32	150
Edmund-street Mission (*Mr. Paginton, L.C.M.*)	30	86	26	50
Wesleyan—				
South-street Mission, Peckham (*Mr. Charles Scales.*)	53	—	60	100
Mission Hall, Hindman's-road (*Mr. R. B. Telfer.*)	—	—	70	500
Stafford-street Mission, Peckham (*Mr. A. B. C. Hesk.*)	—	—	113	250
Presbyterian—				
Camberwell Presbyterian Mission (*Mr. J. Reid Howatt.*)	—	—	125	—
Friends—				
Albert-road Hall, Peckham (*Mr. H. G. Tollett.*)	—	—	{ 70 / 56 }	240
London City Mission—				
Camberwell Hall, Grove-lane (*Mr. C. Steinitz; Mr. G. Robinson.*)	128	—	50	120
Leipsic-road Mission (*Mr. J. Coles.*)	—	—	119	200
Kimpton-road Mission (*Mr. George Robinson.*)	—	—	61	150
Salvation Army—				
George-st., Salvation Army (*Capt. Barrett.*)	{ 7 a.m. 67 / 11 a.m. 300 }	1500	2500	2500
Nunhead Salvation Army (*Capt. D. T. Thomas.*)	{ 7 a.m. 30 / 11 a.m. 86 }	130	200	180
West Peckham, Sal. Army (*Capt. Cooper.*)	{ 7 a.m. 39 / 10.30 a.m. 108 }	147	350	350
Undenominational—				
Peckham Public Hall (*Mr. T. J. Field.*)	—	400	325	1100
Alders-street Mission, Peckham (*Miss R. Fuller.*)	13	-	23	50

MISSION HALLS—GREENWICH.

Missions.	Morning.	Afternoon.	Evening.	Accom.
Undenominational (*continued*)—				
Caroline-street Mission, Old Kent-rd.	33	—	199	—
(*Mr. G. Hatt.*)				
Mission, 104, Lower Park-rd., Peckham	—	—	—	165
(*Mr. L. Wood.*)				
Kirkwood-road Mission, Peckham Rye	—	—	45	70
(*Mr. J. S. Eidman, Jun.*)				
Welcome Mis., Camberwell New-road	—	—	50	60
(*Mr. G. H. Cracknell.*)				
Surrey Masonic Hall	—	174	—	250
(*Mr. A. Wickson, Hon. Sec.*)				
Albany Hall, 45, Albany-road	—	—	168	270
(*Mr. J. T. Stickley; Mr. White.*)				
Beresford Mission Hall, Crown-street	—	55	115	—

GREENWICH.

Comprising the Sub-Districts of St. Paul, Deptford; St. Nicholas; Greenwich West; Greenwich East.

Missions.	Morning.	Afternoon.	Evening.	Accom.
Church of England—				
St. John's Mission Hall, King-street	84	—	231	300
(*Rev. E. J. Hone.*)				
Deptford Mission Room	—	—	—	300
(*Rev. J. B. Drake.*)				
Cold Bath-street Mission, Greenwich	—	—	109	—
(*Rev. E. C. Gedge.*)				
St. Paul's Mission, Roan-street	—	No service	—	100
(*Rev. A. Love.*)				
Chester-street Mission Hall	—	—	55	50
Congregational—				
Tanner's Hill Mission	—	—	202	225
(*Rev. J. Morley Wright; Mr. Fairbank.*)				
Payne-street, Deptford	—	—	35	—
(*Rev. J. Morley Wright; Rev. W. Robinson.*)				
Napier-street Hall, Deptford	159	—	190	220
(*Rev. J. Morley Wright; Rev. W. Robinson.*)				
E. Greenwich, Lnthrp. and Armtge.-rds.	180	—	205	350
(*Mr. A. J. England.*)				
Ragged-school Mission, High-street	—	—	55	250
(*Mr. Hackerton.*)				
Baptist—				
Creek-street Mission Hall, Deptford	—	58	90	40
(*Mr. J. M. Wigner.*)				
Working Men's Mission, Roan-street	—	—	259	300
(*Mr. J. Newman.*)				
Caletock-street Hall	—	—	53	800
(*Mr. W. Beer.*)				

THE RELIGIOUS CENSUS OF LONDON.

MISSIONS.	MORN-ING.	AFTER-NOON.	EVEN-ING.	AC-COM.
Wesleyan—				
Mission, Trafalgar-road	—	—	300	450
(*Rev. T. Derry.*)				
Presbyterian—				
Blisset-street Mission	—	—	86	100
Brethren—				
George-street Hall	160	60	400	500
Lecture Hall, Royal Hill	—	—	356	—
(*Mr. Samuel Sims.*)				
Friends—				
Friends' Meeting House, Deptford	17	—	41	230
London City Mission—				
Evelyn Mission Hall, Staunton	—	—	57	200
(*Mr. Couch.*)				
Three Cups Coffee Tavern	—	—	105	140
(*Mr. Saberton.*)				
Evelyn-street Mission, Deptford	—	—	75	100
(*Mr. J. Smith.*)				
Randal-place, Roan-street, Greenwich	—	—	130	160
(*Mr. J. Crowther, Supt.*)				
Hall, 284, Devons-road, Bow Common	—	—	50	100
(*Mr. Parsons.*)				
Mission, Charles-street, Deptford	—	—	60	90
(*Mr. W. Bennett.*)				
George Livesay's Inst., Blackwall-lane	—	—	65	100
(*Mr. T. Woodman.*)				
Undenominational—				
Thames Mission, River-terrace	—	—	46	125
South Eastern Raily. Mission, New Cross	21	—	25	100
(*Mr. E. C. Cox, Hon. Sec.*)				
New-street, Deptford	179	—	150	300
Upper East-street, Greenwich	—	—	280	350
(*Mr. H. Platt.*)				

LEWISHAM.

COMPRISING THE SUB-DISTRICTS OF ELTHAM, LEE, LEWISHAM VILLAGE, SYDENHAM.

	MORN-ING.	AFTER-NOON.	EVEN-ING.	AC-COM.
Church of England—				
Bennett-st. Mission Room, Coldbath	—	—	105	200
(*Rev. E. L. Gedge.*)				
Congregational—				
Nightingale-grove Mission	—	—	70	200
(*Rev. J. M. Jones.*)				
Mill-lane (Lewisham High-rd. Chapel)	—	—	44	80
(*Rev. J. Morley Wright; Mr. H. Harmsworth.*)				

MISSION HALLS—WOOLWICH.

Missions.	Morning.	Afternoon.	Evening.	Accom.
Congregational (*continued*)—				
Lewisham Congregational Mission	—	—	—	120
(*Rev. J. M. Jones.*)				
Ladywell Mission	—	—	50	250
(*Rev. J. M. Jones.*)				
Park Hall, Sydenham	—	—	20	300
(*Mr. P. Eldridge, L.C.M.*)				
Rushey-green Mission	—	—	70	100
(*Mr. Wheeler.*)				
Baptist—				
Bell-green Mission, Sydenham	—	—	68	220
(*Mr. W. H. Griffen.*)				
Burnt Ash Mission Hall	52	—	60	200
Wesleyan—				
Merritt-road, Brockley	—	—	34	50
(*Mr. Page; Major Mellor, Sec.*)				
Lower Sydenham Mission	60	—	—	150
(*Rev. H. Douthwaite.*)				
Brethren—				
Court Hill Hall	45	—	53	200
Alexandra Hall, Bennett-park	220	125	300	420
(*Dr. McKillian.*)				
London City Mission—				
Coldbath Mission	—	—	30	80
(*Mr. Horobin.*)				
Salvation Army—				
21, Vian Street, Lewisham	7 a.m. 13 / 11 a.m. 63	95	129	120
(*Capt. A. Weedon.*)				
Undenominational—				
Mission Hall, Shrubbery-road	—	—	113	140
(*Mr. J. Roberts.*)				
Christian Mission Hall, Coombe-road	40	—	100	200
Canonbury Hall, Lewisham	82	33	190	200
(*Mr. R. Turner.*)				
Lecture Hall, Sydenham	—	—	25	40
(*Mr. J. F. Taylor.*)				

WOOLWICH.

Comprising the Sub-Districts of Charlton, Woolwich Dockyard, Woolwich Arsenal, Plumstead West, Plumstead East.

Missions.	Morning.	Afternoon.	Evening.	Accom.
Church of England—				
St. John's Mission Hall, Ordnance-rd.	—	—	85	150
(*Rev. Edmund Kimber.*)				
St. Mary's Mission, Woolwich	—	113	120	130
(*Mr. H. Hame, Lay Reader.*)				

Missions.	Morning.	Afternoon.	Evening.	Accom.
Baptist—				
Conduit-road Chapel, Plumstead	124	—	153	600
(*Rev. C. W. Townsend.*)				
Joseph-street Chapel, Woolwich	20	—	36	200
(*Rev. A. Read.*)				
Assembly Room, New-road	—	850	—	—
(*Rev. J. Wilson.*)				
Co-operative Hall, Powis-street	—	70	—	—
(*Rev. J. Wilson.*)				
New Beckton Mis., North Woolwich	—	—	60	—
(*Rev. J. Wilson.*)				
Powis-street Board School Mission	—	—	110	—
(*Rev. J. Wilson.*)				
Blue Ribbon Mission, Woolwich	—	—	200	—
(*Rev. J. Wilson.*)				
The Slade Mission, Woolwich	—	—	72	150
(*Miss Russell.*)				
Brethren—				
Gospel Hall, Prospect-place	22	—	140	160
Young Men's Christian Association—				
Y.M.C.A., 153, Powis st., Woolwich	—	22	—	40
(*Mr. James Bird, Hon. Sec.*)				
London City Mission—				
Charlton-vale Mission (German)	—	—	24	—
(*Mr. Bottjer.*)				
Mis. Room, 125, Anne-st., Plumstead	—	—	53	50
(*Mr. Thomas Phipps.*)				
Salvation Army—				
Salvation Army, Woolwich Corps { 7 a.m. 35 { 11 a.m. 239		420	776	800
(*Capt. Wharton.*)				
Undenominational—				
Cage-lane Mission Hall, Plumstead	—	—	320	400
(*Miss Russell.*)				
Soldiers' Home, Hill-street	—	—	140	300
(*Mrs. Dent.*)				
Mission Math. Inst. Wks., Charlton	—	—	74	300
(*Mr. J. Simms.*)				
Cromwell House, 85, Beresford-street	—	—	25	—
(*Mr. H. Bristow Wallen.*)				
Mission Room, 30, Ordnance-road	—	—	91	150
(*Mr. Lush.*)				

Printed by Hazell, Watson & Viney, Ld., London and Aylesbury.

Every Friday.   *Price One Penny.*

THE BRITISH WEEKLY.

A Journal of Christian and Social Progress.

PRINCIPAL FEATURES:—

Leading Article.
Tempted London.   Notes of the Week.
A Serial Story.
The Correspondence of Claudius Clear.
Personal.
Rambling Remarks by a Man of Kent.
News of the Churches.
Pulpit Notes.   British Table Talk.
Sketches by Gavin Ogilvy.

RECENT NOTICES OF THE PRESS.

"By far the ablest and most readable of all the religious weeklies."—*Methodist Recorder.*

"The ablest of all the religious weeklies, and in many ways a pattern for the rest."—*Newcastle Leader.*

"A stream of the best religious literature of every land flows into our editorial sanctum, and thence, after being duly filtered, fills the columns of the *Southern Cross*. Religious papers everywhere, with scarcely an exception, grow brighter and wider, more tolerant and more vigorous; but the brightest and widest, the most tolerant and most vigorous, of all our exchanges is, perhaps, THE BRITISH WEEKLY. THE BRITISH WEEKLY is far and away the most scholarly of popular religious papers, and it is also the most resolutely evangelical."—Melbourne *Southern Cross.*

Post free for Six Months, 3s. 3d.; Twelve Months, 6s. 6d. From the Publishers, 27, Paternoster Row, London.

The British Weekly Pulpit.

A COMPANION JOURNAL TO "THE BRITISH WEEKLY."

Containing specially reported Sermons, Sermon Outlines, Sermonettes for Children, Short Expositions, etc., etc.

EVERY FRIDAY.   **PRICE ONE PENNY.**

LONDON: HODDER & STOUGHTON, 27, PATERNOSTER ROW.

HODDER & STOUGHTON'S

LIST OF ILLUSTRATED AND OTHER GIFT BOOKS.

The Five Shilling Series of Gift Books.

Handsomely bound in cloth, gilt edges, demy 8vo, price 5s. each. With Illustrations.

I.

ALL TRUE. Records of Peril and Adventure by Sea and Land—Remarkable Escapes and Deliverances—Wonders of Nature and Providence, etc. By Dr. JAMES MACAULAY. Twelve Illustrations. Tenth Thousand.

II.

WONDERFUL STORIES of Daring, Peril, and Adventure. By Dr. JAMES MACAULAY. With Full-page Illustrations.

III.

THRILLING TALES of Enterprise and Peril, Adventure and Heroism. By Dr. JAMES MACAULAY. With Sixteen Full-page Illustrations.

IV.

STIRRING STORIES of Peace and War by Land and Sea. By Dr. JAMES MACAULAY. With Sixteen Full-page Illustrations.

V.

CHARLIE LUCKEN at School and College. By the Rev. H. C. ADAMS, M.A., Author of "For James or George." "Schoolboy Honour," etc. With Eight Full-page Illustrations by J. Finnemore.

VI.

THROWN ON THE WORLD; or, The Scrapes and 'Scapes of Ray and Bertie. By EDWIN HODDER, Author of "Tossed on the Waves," etc. With Full-page Illustrations by Gordon Browne.

VII.

FRITZ AND ERIC: The Brother Crusoes. By J. C. HUTCHESON, Author of "The Wreck of the Nancy Bell," "Picked up at Sea." etc. With Full-page Illustrations by Gordon Browne.

VIII.

SOME OF OUR FELLOWS. A School Story. By the Rev. T. S. MILLINGTON, M.A. With Sixteen Full-page Illustrations.

IX.

FROM LOG CABIN TO WHITE HOUSE; The Story of President Garfield's Life. By W. M. THAYER. With Twenty Illustrations and Two Portraits.

Five Shilling Stories.

THE WILLOUGHBY CAPTAINS. A School Story. By TALBOT BAINES REED, Author of "My Friend Smith," "The Fifth Form at St. Dominic's," etc. With Twelve Full-page Illustrations. Crown 8vo, cloth, 5s.

"Boys have here a story to their hearts' content."—*Daily News.*

FROM POWDER MONKEY TO ADMIRAL. A Story of Naval Adventure. By W. H. G. KINGSTON. Eight Illustrations. Eighth Thousand. Gilt edges, 5s.

"Kingston's tales require no commendation. They are full of go. All lads enjoy them, and many men. This is one of his best stories—a youthful critic assures us his very best."—*Sheffield Independent.*

PETER TRAWL; or, The Adventures of a Whaler. With Eight Illustrations. By the same Author. Fifth Thousand. Crown 8vo, gilt edges, 5s.

"Here will be found shipwrecks and desert islands, and hair-breadth escapes of every kind, all delightful and spirit-stirring."—*Court Journal.*

"It is a manly sort of book, with a good deal of information in it, as well as the adventures which boys love."—*Athenæum.*

TRUE TALES of Travel and Adventure, Valour and Virtue. By DR. JAMES MACAULAY. With Thirteen Illustrations. Fifth Thousand. Crown 8vo, cloth, 5s.

"Dr. Macaulay's name is a voucher for spirited work, and 'True Tales' are instructive as well as interesting."—*Times.*

IN THE DEPTHS OF THE SEA. By OLD BOOMERANG. With Frontispiece. Crown 8vo, gilt edges, 5s.

THE PIONEER OF A FAMILY; or, Adventures of a Young Governess. By the same Author. Second Edition. With Frontispiece. Gilt edges, 5s.

"Few stories have such an air of reality about them. Mr. Hawthorn has the faculty of drawing his characters in such graphic fashion, that we seem to have known them, and are forced to sympathise with their joys and sorrows."—*Aberdeen Free Press.*

"Full of terse and powerful sketches of colonial life."—*Freeman.*

JOSEPH HATTON'S NEW STORY.

CAPTURED BY CANNIBALS. Some Incidents in the Life of Horace Durand. By JOSEPH HATTON, Author of "Cruel London," "Three Recruits," "The Old House at Sandwich," etc. With Eight Original Illustrations Drawn by W. H. MARGETSON. Crown 8vo, gilt edges, 5s.

EXTRACT FROM THE AUTHOR'S DEDICATORY PREFACE :

"A story that takes its hero into the perils of certain unrecorded countries within easy range of the great island of Borneo, founded upon a careful study of true histories, upon private letters and despatches, and upon the experience of travellers whom I had personally known ; and so real was the result, that I had a long letter from Mr. Pryer voluntarily informing me that my descriptions of the scenery of the islands of the Eastern seas, and my accounts of the native inhabitants of such as had been visited by modern explorers, were so truthful, that it was hard to believe I had not spent much of my life on the Equator. Last year I had long talks with Mr. Pryer, during his brief trip to Europe, when he confirmed by sundry illustrations the truth of his letter, adding that there is not a single incident of 'Captured by Cannibals' which might not have happened."

HARRY MILVAINE ; or, the Wanderings of a Wayward Boy. By Dr. GORDON STABLES, R.N., Author of "The Cruise of the Snowbird," etc. With Full-page Illustrations. 6s.

DR. GORDON STABLES' NEW STORY.

WILD LIFE IN THE LAND OF THE GIANTS. A Tale of Two Brothers. By GORDON STABLES, M.D., C.M., Author of "Wild Adventures Round the Pole," "Harry Milvaine," "The Cruise of the Snowbird," etc. With Cover Designed by W. H. MARGETSON, and Eight Illustrations. 8vo, gilt edges, 6s.

THE AUTHOR SAYS :

"The story is intended to describe, in a racy and readable form, the wild sports and adventures one meets with in the Patagonian Pampas and the Straits of Magellan, betwixt Patagonia and Tierra del Fuego—the land of fire

"The adventures at home are nearly all painted from the life. For instance, the story of the thunderbolt and poor Tom Morley's sad death is true.

"The great love the twin brothers had for each other is carried through the story, and rests on a strange psychological fact, that twins sometimes seem animated by the same thoughts and feelings precisely as if their very souls were one.

"The adventures are all exciting without being horrible. The tale is healthy and manly without being goody-goody."

Five Shilling Stories.

VERMONT HALL; or, Light through the Darkness. By M. A. PAULL (Mrs. John Ripley), Author of "The Flower of the Grassmarket," etc. With Eight Illustrations. Crown 8vo, cloth, 5s.

ON SPECIAL SERVICE: A Tale of Life at Sea. By GORDON STABLES, M.D., R.N. With Eight Full-page Illustrations by J. Finnemore. Handsomely bound in cloth, gilt edges, 5s.

MORE TRUE THAN TRUTHFUL. A Story by C. M. CLARKE. With Eight Illustrations. Crown 8vo, cloth, 5s.

STEPPING HEAVENWARD. By Mrs. PRENTISS. With Eight Full-page Illustrations, printed in monotint. Handsomely bound in cloth, 5s.

HOW IT ALL CAME ROUND. By L. T. MEADE. With Six Illustrations. Handsomely bound, 5s.

"A charming story. The characters are excellently drawn."—*Standard*.

"The story is worthy of the highest praise. Altogether, this is one of the best stories of the season."—*Pall Mall Gazette*.

THE WHITE CROSS AND DOVE OF PEARLS. A Biography of Light and Shade. By S. C. INGHAM. Seventh Thousand. Crown 8vo, cloth, 5s.

YENSIE WALTON'S WOMANHOOD. By J. R. GRAHAM CLARK. With Three Illustrations. Crown 8vo, cloth, 5s.

THE OWNERS OF BROADLANDS. By Mrs. H. B. PAULL. With Full-page Illustrations. Crown 8vo, cloth, 5s.

THE SISTERS OF GLENCOE; or, Letitia's Choice By EVA WYNNE. Twenty-second Thousand. Crown 8vo, cloth elegant, 5s.

"Its life pictures are skilfully drawn, and the most wholesome lessons are enforced with fidelity and power."—*Temperance Record*.

"An admirable story, illustrating in a most effective manner the mischief arising from the use of intoxicating liquors."—*Rock*.

Five Shilling Stories.

BY A WAY SHE KNEW NOT. The Story of Allison Bain. By MARGARET M. ROBERTSON, Author of "Christie Redfern's Troubles," etc. With Eight Illustrations by G. H. EDWARDS. Crown 8vo, cloth, 5s.

THE BAIRNS; or, Janet's Love and Service. With Five Illustrations. Thirteenth Thousand. Crown 8vo, cloth elegant, 5s.

"A special interest attaches to 'The Bairns.' The characters are forcibly delineated, and the touches of homeliness which seem almost peculiar to our northern kinsfolk impart a peculiar charm."—*Record.*

MEG'S MISTAKE, and other Sussex Stories. By MRS. O'REILLY. With Twenty Illustrations by Fred. Barnard. Crown 8vo, cloth, 5s.

"We have never seen better stories of their kind."—*Academy.*

A ROUND OF SUNDAY STORIES. By L. G. SÉGUIN. With numerous Illustrations by F. A. Fraser, Fred. Barnard, etc. Handsomely bound in cloth, 5s.

"They are brief, bright, and illustrated with excellent woodcuts. It is the kind of book often earnestly desired when, on a wet Sabbath, the children are restless and beg to have something read to amuse them. Then such a work as this seems of priceless value."—*Freeman.*

IN A CORNER OF THE VINEYARD. A Village Story. By TIGHE HOPKINS (ISAAC PLEYDELL). With Frontispiece. Crown 8vo, 5s.

"The hard, rough life of the men is vigorously drawn."—*Athenæum.*

BY THE AUTHOR OF "THE CHILDREN OF INDIA," etc.

THE CHILDREN OF AFRICA: Written for all English-Speaking Children. With Map and Numerous Illustrations. Fcap. 4to, handsomely bound in cloth, gilt edges, 5s.

THE CHILDREN OF CHINA: Written for the Children of England. By the same Author. With Numerous Illustrations. Handsomely bound, fcap. 4to, gilt edges, 5s.

"Will be joyfully welcomed. Well written, very elegantly bound, and profusely illustrated, with a good map at the beginning. We have seldom seen a book for children which we liked better, or could more heartily recommend as a prize or present."—*Record.*

BY A WAY SHE KNEW NOT.

Specimen of the Illustrations.

Girls' Select Library.

Handsomely bound in cloth, crown 8vo, price 3s. 6d. each, gilt edges.

AN ANGEL GUEST IN HUMAN GUISE. By RUTH LAMB, Author of "Alice Western's Blessing," etc. With Frontispiece by J. Finnemore.

THE TWA MISS DAWSONS. By the Author of "Christie Redfern's Troubles," etc.

THEODORA CAMERON. A Home Story. By PHŒBE J. MCKEEN. With Five Full-page Illustrations.

THE BELLS OF DUMBARTON. By LUCY LINCOLN MONTGOMERY. With Three Illustrations.

NIGEL LENNOX OF GLEN IRVINE. By L. N. HYDER. With Five Full-page Illustrations.

DESSIE FENNIMORE. By Miss HUTTON, Author of "Holiday Time at Forest House," etc.

A LONG LANE WITH A TURNING. A Story. By SARAH DOUDNEY. With Sixteen Illustrations by M. E. EDWARDS.

NOTHING BUT LEAVES. By SARAH DOUDNEY.

THE TRUE WOMAN. Elements of Character drawn from the Life of Mary Lyon and others. By W. M. THAYER, Author of "From Log Cabin to White House," "The Pioneer Boy," etc.

DAISY SNOWFLAKE'S SECRET. A Story of English Home Life. By Mrs. G. S. REANEY.

JUST IN TIME; or, Howard Clarion's Rescue. By the same Author.

INGLESIDE; or, Without Christ and With Him. By Mrs. MADELINE LESLIE, Author of "Tim, the Scissors Grinder," etc. With Five Illustrations.

LAURA LINWOOD. By S. C. INGHAM, Author of "The White Cross and Dove of Pearls." With Frontispiece.

Girls' Select Library—*continued.*

WHAT'S IN A NAME? By SARAH DOUDNEY. With Eight Illustrations.

PRUDENCE WINTERBURN. By the same Author. With Eight Illustrations.

THE FLOWER OF THE GRASSMARKET. By M A. PAULL RIPLEY, Author of "Tim's Troubles," etc. With Five Full-page Illustrations.

CLUNY MACPHERSON. A Tale of Brotherly Love. By A. E. BARR, Author of "Jan Vedder's Wife," etc.

THE PENNANT FAMILY. The Story of the Earl of Craigavon. By ANNE BEALE, Author of "Gladys the Reaper," etc. With Eight Full-page Illustrations.

Boys' Select Library.

Handsomely bound in cloth, crown 8vo, gilt edges, price **3s. 6d.** each.

THE CRUISE OF THE "SNOWBIRD." A Story of Arctic Adventure. By DR. GORDON STABLES, R.N. With Nine Full-page Illustrations.

FROM POLE TO POLE. A Tale of the Sea. By the same Author. With Twelve Full-page Illustrations.

ANDREW MARVEL AND HIS FRIENDS: A Story of the Siege of Hull. By MARIE HALL. Fourth Thousand.

FOR JAMES OR GEORGE? A Schoolboy's Tale of 1745. By the Rev. H. C. ADAMS, M.A., Author of "Schoolboy Honour," etc. With Twelve Full-page Illustrations.

MARTIN LUTHER: Student, Monk, Reformer. By JOHN RAE, LL.D., F.S.A. With Six Illustrations.

AFRICA, PAST AND PRESENT. A Concise Account of the Country and its People. By AN OLD RESIDENT. With Map and Illustrations.

TOSSED ON THE WAVES. A Story of Young Life. By EDWIN HODDER. Seventeenth Thousand.

Boys' Select Library—*continued.*

JAMES BRAITHWAITE, THE SUPERCARGO. The Story of his Adventures Ashore and Afloat. By W. H. G. KINGSTON. Author of "From Powder Monkey to Admiral," etc. With Eight Full-page Illustrations, Portrait, and Short Account of the Author.

HENDRICKS THE HUNTER; or, The Border Farm. A Tale of Zululand. By W. H. G. KINGSTON. With Five Full-page Illustrations.

ORIENT BOYS: A Tale of School Life.

A BRAVE RESOLVE; or, The Siege of Stralsund. A Story of Heroism and Adventure. By J. B. DE LIEFDE, Author of "The Great Dutch Admirals," etc. With Eight Full-page Illustrations.

THE BEGGARS; or, The Founders of the Dutch Republic. By the same Author. With Four Illustrations.

WILD ADVENTURES ROUND THE POLE; or, The Cruise of the "Snowbird" Crew in the "Arrandoon." By Dr. GORDON STABLES, R.N. With Eight Illustrations.

SUCCESSFUL MEN who have Risen from the Ranks. By SARAH K. BOLTON. Eight Portraits.

SHORE AND SEA. Stories of Great Vikings and Sea Captains. By W. H. DAVENPORT ADAMS. Ten Illustrations.

GREY HAWK: Life and Adventures among the Red Indians. An Old Story Retold. By Dr. JAMES MACAULAY, Author of "Thrilling Tales," "All True," "Wonderful Stories," etc. With Eleven Illustrations.

LAUNCHING AWAY; or, Roger Larksway's Strange Mission. With Frontispiece. By the Author of "The Pioneer of the Family," etc.

Mr. W. M. Thayer's "Log Cabin" Series.

I.

Now Ready. 30th Edition, completing 171st Thousand.

FROM LOG CABIN TO WHITE HOUSE; The Story of President Garfield's Life. In paper boards, illustrated cover, with fine steel portrait, 1s.; in cloth, 1s. 6d.; gilt edges, 2s.: cloth gilt, 2s. 6d, and 3s 6d.; illustrated edition, gilt edges, 5s.

"One of the most romantic stories of our time."—*British Quarterly Review.*

II.

THE PIONEER BOY, and HOW HE BECAME PRESIDENT; The Story of the Life of Abraham Lincoln. Many of the details of this work were furnished by PRESIDENT LINCOLN himself, and by his early associates and friends. Cheap Edition. Sixteenth Thousand, 3s. 6d., with Portrait.

"Mr. Thayer is not merely a biographer, a compiler of dry details, but he invests his subject with a halo of delightful romance, and the result is as pleasing as the most imaginative book of fiction. So cleverly has the author done his work, that the result is a combination of pictures from the life of this great man, with humorous anecdote and stirring narrative."—*Society.*

III.

GEORGE WASHINGTON: His Boyhood and Manhood. Cheap Edition. Tenth Thousand, 3s. 6d., with Steel Portrait.

"The character of Washington was a very noble one, and his life may well be taken as an example by boys. The biography is written in a lively and pleasant tone, and without any of the dryness which is too often the accompaniment of this form of literature. While the details are all strictly historical, the characters are made to live and breathe."—*Standard.*

IV.

FROM THE TANYARD TO WHITE HOUSE; The Story of President Grant's Life. With portrait and illustrations. Nineteenth Thousand. Crown 8vo, cloth, 3s. 6d. and 2s. 6d.

"General Grant's romantic and noble story is here popularly told with great effectiveness. Mr. Thayer seems destined to be the popular historian of American presidents—Washington, Lincoln, and Garfield have already been portrayed by his pen, and now in General Grant he has found a hero second to none of them. He has many high qualifications for his task. The book is one of romantic and enthralling interest."—*British Quarterly Review.*

BY THE SAME AUTHOR.

TACT, PUSH, AND PRINCIPLE; A Book for those who wish to Succeed in Life. Fourteenth Thousand. Crown 8vo, cloth, 3s. 6d.

"A very interesting book, which may stimulate many a young nature of the ardently practical kind to steady and determined exertion."—*Daily Telegraph.*

CAPITAL FOR WORKING BOYS. Chapters on Character Building. By J. E. M'CONAUGHY. Crown 8vo, cloth, 3s. 6d.

Stories at 3s. 6d.

FIVE LITTLE PEPPERS, AND HOW THEY GREW. By MARGARET SIDNEY. With humorous Illustrations. Crown 8vo, cloth, 3s. 6d.

"One of the brightest and most cheerful books we have ever read. Full of fun and life."—*Christian World.*

COST WHAT IT MAY. By Mrs. E. E. HORNIBROOK. With Illustrations. Crown 8vo, cloth, 3s. 6d.

"Among the cartloads of boneless, nerveless fiction that are tumbled out of our modern presses, it is truly refreshing to meet with such a charming book as this. It is really a gem of literature worthy to be possessed both by young men and maidens."—*Christian.*

CANDALARIA. A Heroine of the Wild West. By Mrs. J. A. OWEN, Author of "Our Honolulu Boys," etc. With Eight Full-page Illustrations. Crown 8vo, cloth, 3s. 6d.

"A pleasantly-written story of love and adventure, with a charming heroine."—*Bradford Observer.*

A SON OF THE MORNING. By SARAH DOUDNEY. With Frontispiece. 3s. 6d.

"It is a work of high art, of high literary quality, full of high feeling, knowledge of human nature, keen insight into human character. It is quite a gem of a novelette, and will be a favourite, not with young readers alone and not with one set alone."—*School Board Chronicle.*

WHEN WE WERE GIRLS TOGETHER. By the same Author. With Four Full-page Illustrations. Crown 8vo, cloth, 3s. 6d.

"A clever story. From first to last the interest is well sustained."—*City Press.*

EUNICE. By the Author of "Christie Redfern's Troubles," etc. With Eight Illustrations. Crown 8vo, cloth, 3s. 6d.

"A very bright and pretty story. The characters are well individualised, and Mrs. Stone is really good."—*Academy.*

FREDERICA AND HER GUARDIANS; or, The Perils of Orphanhood. By the same Author. Cheaper Edition. Crown 8vo, cloth, 3s. 6d.

"A sweet, pure, and beautiful story."—*Sheffield Independent.*

Stories at 3s. 6d.

A LITTLE SILVER TRUMPET. By L. T. Meade. With Twelve Illustrations by T. Pym. Crown 8vo, 3s. 6d.

"A delightful book, delightfully illustrated."—*Scotsman.*

NOBLE, BUT NOT THE NOBLEST. By Marie Hall. Crown 8vo, 3s. 6d.

"The picture is skilfully drawn, with tender touches and with artistic lights. We heartily commend it. To those who have read the author's previous stories of 'The Dying Saviour and the Gipsy Girl,' 'Andrew Marvel,' etc., this is scarcely necessary."—*British Quarterly Review.*

"A more elegantly written, graceful, and powerful story the present season has not yielded us."—*Freeman.*

THE DYING SAVIOUR AND THE GIPSY GIRL, and other Tales. By the same Author. Sixteenth Thousand. Crown 8vo, cloth, 3s. 6d.

"The stories are gracefully written: they are marked by good feeling and refined taste, and the moral conveyed by them is unexceptionable."—*Spectator.*

OLIVER WYNDHAM. A Tale of the Great Plague. By the Author of "Naomi; or, The Last Days of Jerusalem," etc. Fifteenth Thousand. Crown 8vo, cloth, 3s. 6d.

THE BOY IN THE BUSH. A Tale of Australian Life. By Richard Rowe. With Illustrations. Crown 8vo, 3s. 6d.

"Young lads will feel the narrative of the dash and courage of colonial boys of from ten to fourteen to be exhilarating reading."—*School Board Chronicle.*

DAVID LIVINGSTONE: The Story of his Life and Labours; or, The Weaver Boy who became a Missionary. By H. G. Adams. With Steel Portrait and Thirty Illustrations. Sixty-first Thousand. Crown 8vo, cloth, 3s. 6d.

"An admirable condensation of 'The Story of the Life and Labours of Dr. Livingstone.' Comprehensive in range, abounding in detail, and vividly presenting the graphic description of the great explorer himself."—*Record.*

BY L. T. MEADE.

I.

THE AUTOCRAT OF THE NURSERY. With Forty Illustrations by T. Pym. Fcap. 4to, handsomely bound, 3s. 6d.

"We have seldom seen a more spirited and delightful story for little children."—*Guardian.*

"A most charming children's story, exquisitely illustrated."—*Truth.*

"ON CLOTHES-HORSES."

II.

THE ANGEL OF LOVE. A Companion Volume to "The Autocrat of the Nursery." With Forty Illustrations by T. Pym. Fcap. 4to, handsomely bound, 3s. 6d.

THE CHILDREN'S PASTIME: Pictures and Stories.
By L. G. Séguin. With 200 Illustrations. Square crown 8vo, 3s. 6d.

STORY AFTER STORY of Land and Sea, Man and Beast.
By the Author of "Sunday Evenings with my Children," etc. With 130 Illustrations. Square crown 8vo, cloth, 3s. 6d.

"For young people this volume must prove quite an attractive mine of amusement. It will make an excellent prize."—*Schoolmaster.*

"A most attractive and useful volume for young readers."—*Rock.*

CHEERFUL SUNDAYS: Stories, Parables, and Poems for Children. By the same Author. With 150 Illustrations. Square crown 8vo, 3s. 6d.

"'Cheerful Sundays' is the title of another volume of religious stories and verses for children. It is well done, and is excellently illustrated."—*Scotsman.*

"A good book for Sunday reading for little ones."—*Standard.*

OUR BROTHERS AND SONS. By Mrs. G. S. Reaney. Fifth Thousand. Elegantly bound, 3s. 6d.

"One of her best books, written in excellent English, and with a racy, earnest pen."—*Evangelical Magazine.*

HERMIE'S ROSEBUDS, and other Stories. By L. T. Meade. With Illustrations. Handsomely bound, 3s. 6d.

THE STORY OF THE LIFE OF JESUS Told in Words Easy to Read and Understand. By the Author of "The Story of the Bible," etc. With Forty Illustrations. Handsomely bound, fcap. 4to, cloth, 1s. 6d.

"An excellent Sunday book for children; the story is tenderly and brightly told, the pictures of Eastern life and Jewish manners form an effective running commentary on the text, which is interspersed besides with graphic views of the sacred cities, sites, and scenery."—*Times.*

The Ivy Stories.

Handsomely bound in cloth, 2s., gilt edges, 2s. 6d., illustrated.

THE RED HOUSE IN THE SUBURBS. By Mrs. O'REILLY, Author of "Meg's Mistake," etc. With Twenty-six Illustrations by F. A. Fraser.

THE WINTHROP FAMILY. A Story of New England Life Fifty Years Ago. By the Author of "May Chester," etc.

COMRADES. A Story. By SARAH TYTLER. With Illustrations.

IN THE FORT. By the same Author. With Frontispiece by J. Finnemore.

LYLE HARCOURT. By A. E. W., Author of "Soldier Harold," etc. With Four Illustrations.

UNCLE TOM'S CABIN. With Four Illustrations. By HARRIET BEECHER STOWE.

THE PRINCE OF THE HOUSE OF DAVID; or, Three Years in the Holy City. Edited by the Rev. PROFESSOR J. H. INGRAHAM. With Five Illustrations.

STRAWBERRY HILL. By CLARA VANCE, Author of "Andy Luttrell," etc. With Four Illustrations.

TALBURY GIRLS. By the same Author. Four Illustrations.

THE JUDGE'S SONS. A Story of Wheat and Tares. With Four Illustrations.

BARBARA. A Story of Cloud and Sunshine. By CLARA VANCE. Four Illustrations.

SUKIE'S BOY. A Story by SARAH TYTLER, Author of "Comrades," "In the Fort," etc. With Four Illustrations.

www.ingramcontent.com/pod-product-compliance
Lightning Source LLC
Chambersburg PA
CBHW022138160426
43197CB00009B/1340